TILTING

TILTING

HOUSE LAUNCHING, SLIDE HAULING, POTATO TRENCHING,

AND OTHER TALES FROM A
NEWFOUNDLAND FISHING VILLAGE

ROBERT MELLIN

PRINCETON ARCHITECTURAL PRESS

NEW YORK

For Heidi, Julia, and Hannah

Published by
Princeton Architectural Press
37 East Seventh Street
New York, New York 10003

For a free catalog of books, call 1.800.722.6657.
Visit our Web site at www.papress.com.

All photographs and drawings © Robert Mellin unless otherwise indicated.
Page II: Aerial view of Tilting, early 1990s (photo courtesy
Newfoundland and Labrador Air Photo and Map Library)

Editing: Clare Jacobson
Editorial assistance: Megan Carey and Nicola Bednarek
Design: Deb Wood

Special thanks to: Nettie Aljian, Ann Alter, Janet Behning, Penny Chu,
Russell Fernandez, Jan Haux, Mark Lamster, Nancy Eklund Later,
Linda Lee, Katharine Myers, Jane Sheinman, Scott Tennent, and
Jennifer Thompson of Princeton Architectural Press
—Kevin C. Lippert, publisher

Library of Congress Cataloging-in-Publication Data
Mellin, Robert
   Tilting : house launching, slide hauling, potato trenching, and other
tales from a Newfoundland fishing village / Robert Mellin.— 1st ed.
      p. cm.
   Includes bibliographical references and index.
   ISBN 1-56898-383-2 (hard cover : alk. paper)
   1. Architecture, Domestic—Canada—Tilting. 2. Architecture—
Canada—Tilting—English influences. 3. Architecture—Canada—
Tilting—20th century. 4. Architecture—Canada—Tilting—19th
century. 5. Tilting (Canada)—Buildings, structures, etc. 6.Tilting
(Canada)—Social life and customs.   I. Title.
NA7243.T55M45 2003
720'.9718—dc21   2002013707

CONTENTS

Houses and outbuildings on the east side of The Pond

ACKNOWLEDGMENTS

While researching this book, I was fortunate to get to know most of the people in Tilting. They welcomed me into their lives and generously informed me about the structures and artifacts they made, and about how these related to their way of life. I have since come to know these people as my neighbors, and my family has been made to feel as though they are part of Tilting's many extended families. We try to return to Tilting every year to renew our friendships and to experience something very different from our urban life in St. John's and Montreal. Though the old ways are disappearing, some of the practices as well as the memories remain. I would find it nearly impossible to list all the many people who befriended and assisted me in Tilting, but special mention must be made of Ambrose and Gladys McGrath's family, and Pearce and Doreen Dwyer's family. They are my families away from home.

The timing of my first visit to Tilting was fortuitous. The village was experiencing major changes in employment, lifestyle, demographics, architecture, and settlement patterns, but I found there were many residents who had a remarkable knowledge of local history and customs. They helped me immeasurably by consenting to long interviews, often taking time away from their daily work. Although I cannot list all the persons I interviewed here, I must express my thanks to Margaret Broaders, Dorothy Burke, Fergus Burke, Rose Burke, Stella Burke, Ted Burke, Terry Burke, Albert and Philomena Cluett, Gertrude Dwyer, Gilbert Dwyer, Pearce and Doreen Dwyer, Ben and Annie Foley, Clarence and Philomena Foley, Alice Greene, Dan Greene, Jim Greene, Martin Greene, Mike Greene, Allan and Mary Keefe, Val Kinsella, Mike Lane, Gladys McGrath, Edith Reardon, Gerald Reardon, and Mercedes Ryan. I would like to thank Clara Byrne for generously sharing her collection of old photographs of Tilting. I must especially thank Tilting historian Jim McGrath for helping me with my inquiries, and his brothers Andrew, Cyril, Frank, George, Len, Leo, and Neil, as well as their families. They looked out for me, showed me around, and invited me to haul cod traps, to hand line for cod, to journey to Little Fogo Islands, and to make trips to harvest wood on the slide paths.

Fergus Burke   *Martin Greene*   *Pearce Dwyer*   *Rose Burke*

I wish to thank McGill University for providing a grant for my
research on Newfoundland's architecture. Canada Mortgage and
Housing Corporation provided a scholarship for the initial research.
The Heritage Foundation of Newfoundland and Labrador provided
funding to assist with the production of drawings, and the Institute of
Social and Economic Research and the Centre for Material Culture
Studies at Memorial University made me welcome. I am indebted to my
former teacher and distinguished teaching colleague at the School of
Architecture at McGill, Professor Norbert Schoenauer, who encouraged
me to pursue my studies on vernacular architecture. Subsequently, at
the University of Pennsylvania I was very fortunate to study with
Professor Henry Glassie. His inspired studies provided me with new
ways of understanding the complexities of architecture and material
folk culture. Also at Penn, Professor Marco Frascari encouraged me to
interpret Tilting's architecture with drawings, and Professors Peter
McCleary and Robert Blair St. George provided much helpful support
in the early stages of my research.

I am indebted to Professor Gerald Pocius for his advice over the
years. His excellent book on Calvert, Newfoundland set a new standard
for the interpretation of Newfoundland's vernacular architecture.
Professors Shane O'Dea and John Mannion were always willing to
answer my questions and assist with resources and their considerable
insight. John Greene, former resident of Tilting, archivist, author, and
historian, shared invaluable information. My friend Professor William
Barker, head of the Department of English at Memorial University,
provided encouragement to pursue this project and challenged my
ideas. Ruth Canning, chairperson of the Heritage Foundation of

Frank Mahoney

Alice Greene

Newfoundland and Labrador, tirelessly promoted the preservation of Tilting's inshore fishery buildings, as did her brother Stratford. In St. John's, Ned Pratt's expertise was invaluable for the difficult task of photographing the drawings. Joe and Angela Kinsella, Stan Dragland, and Marnie Parsons graciously agreed to review rough manuscripts of this book.

I would especially like to thank Clare Jacobson for her invaluable guidance and superb editing, and Deb Wood for her creative suggestions and inspired design work. My mentors and office mates at McGill, Professors Ricardo Castro and Annmarie Adams, kept me focused on the task at hand with our congenial, almost daily conversations. Not the least of my thanks must go to Professor David Covo, director of the School of Architecture, for giving me the opportunity to teach at McGill University, a position that provided time to revisit my Tilting project.

Finally, I must thank my wife, Heidi, and my children, Julia and Hannah, for their patience with my long absences from home for fieldwork and research.

ROBERT MELLIN, MONTREAL, 2002

I can tell you a joke. Now, me sister Millie, she used to invite us up to dinner Sunday every now and again, and we used to invite her down. So anyway, we put the big roast in the oven in the morning—and potaties and turnip and two lots of pudding, blueberry pudding and a plain pudding—potaties and turnip and cabbage. Anyway, when dinner hour come, Aggie laid the table, I went up for Mill. I said, "Dinner's ready now," so she come down. And—we're just sittin' down—and this knock come to the door. I sung out, "Come in, boy!" And I knows, no one coming for me—I didn't do anything wrong. He said, "Well, you got a wonderful smell." And I said, "Yes, boy." Now he was going around selling vacuum cleaners. I said, "Yes, boy, sit down and join us." And he said, "Me wife is up in the car." And I said, "Go up and tell her to come down and have a pick." I said, "Where are you from?" And he said, "From Gambo"—and he went up and when he comes back he had four more—and Aggie and we sotted at the table and we never got a pick! Now that's as true, my dear man, as you're settin' down there! And Mill used to roar laughing! Well, heavens above—her lovely dinner and never got one pick. Last thing they done, they drank the pot liquor was in the pot with the cabbage—and raved over dinner. And I said, "Yes"—I said, "If ye have done as much knocking around as I've done—you'd be delighted to give them poor people their dinner." I said, "I was glad lots of times for someone to invite me in and give me me dinner." Lots and lots of times—not much odds about it, boy, if we can't help one another—what you gives you'll never miss.

AN ISOLATED NEWFOUNDLAND OUTPORT

ON THE FAR EASTERN EDGE of the North American continent, on a small island eight miles off the northeastern coast of Newfoundland, is the small outport of Tilting, Fogo Island. It is a community of Irish descendents who have been fishing and farming for many generations, and a village I have been documenting since 1987. The architecture of this place is unique: a fragile, ever-transforming architecture that has left few permanent traces on the landscape. It is remarkable that so many of the old houses, outbuildings, and traditional landscape features still exist in Tilting, and I hope that after you read about Tilting's building traditions and way of life, you may travel there yourself one day. Visitors are always welcome in Tilting, and those who have been adventurous enough to trek to this isolated outport have not been disappointed. It is like coming home to another time and another place, where it is impossible to pass someone on the road without saying hello, and where you are always welcome in a warm kitchen for a cup of tea, the wood stove crackling away, kettle on to boil, and where stories, wit, and local history still take priority over television and the Internet.

If you decide to visit Tilting, your sense of its location may depend on your mode of travel.[1] Getting there is not easy, but it is an interesting part of the experience. Intercontinental flights between Europe and North America regularly fly over Newfoundland, oblivious to the island life and landscape six or seven miles below. If you are short of time, you can fly from the mainland or Europe to Newfoundland, either to St. John's or Gander. But the most dramatic itinerary is the approach by sea or by surface from eastern Canada or the eastern United States.

From Montreal it is a two-day trip by car to the northern tip of Cape Breton Island, Nova Scotia. From Boston the duration of the trip is about the same. You then take a six-hour, ocean-going ferry from North Sydney, Nova Scotia to Port-Aux-Basques, Newfoundland. From there you follow the Trans-Canada highway past the western

View of Tilting, 1949, looking towards Pigeon Island. The second church of St. Patrick's Parish is visible on the left. (Photo courtesy Newfoundland and Labrador Aerial Photography Archives)

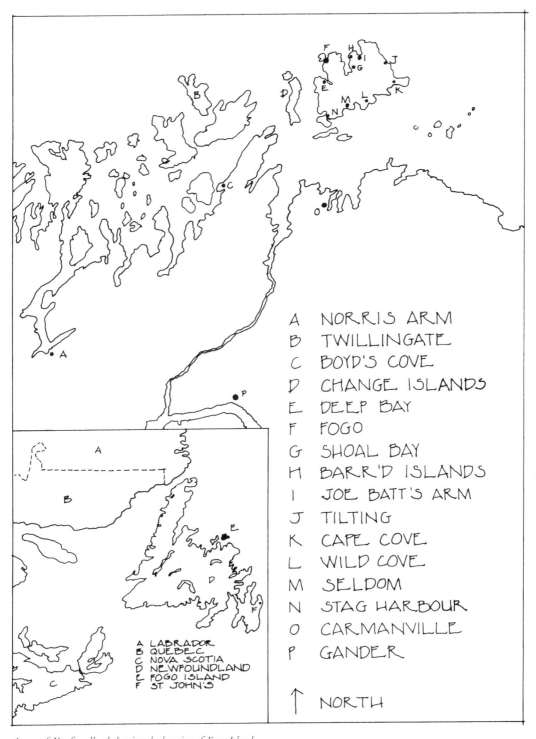

A NORRIS ARM
B TWILLINGATE
C BOYD'S COVE
D CHANGE ISLANDS
E DEEP BAY
F FOGO
G SHOAL BAY
H BARR'D ISLANDS
I JOE BATT'S ARM
J TILTING
K CAPE COVE
L WILD COVE
M SELDOM
N STAG HARBOUR
O CARMANVILLE
P GANDER

↑ NORTH

A LABRADOR
B QUEBEC
C NOVA SCOTIA
D NEWFOUNDLAND
E FOGO ISLAND
F ST. JOHN'S

A map of Newfoundland showing the location of Fogo Island

The Sexton house near Blubber Cove, a light wood-frame house perched on irregular rocky terrain

Newfoundland pulp and paper mill town of Corner Brook, and after seven hours you reach Gander, the international airport town. In the early days of air travel, all trans-Atlantic flights across the North Atlantic had to stop in Gander to refuel. From Gander you drive due north for an hour along Gander Bay, past small fishing communities and old lumber mill towns, until you reach Farewell on Notre Dame Bay, the location of the ferry terminal to Fogo Island. The ferry threads its way through the small Hamilton Sound islands of Farewell Gull Island, North Dog Bay Island, Bons Island, Handy Harbour Island, Woody Island, Western Indian Island, Kate Island, and Indian Lookout Island, until fifty minutes later you arrive in Man-O-War Cove, Fogo Island.

Fogo Island is 15 miles in length and 9 miles wide, and about 120 square miles in area. It is well positioned for access to the fishing grounds of the Notre Dame Bay region. Fogo Island has forested areas along its southern shore, whereas its northern shore is a mostly barren, rocky coast. The Fogo Shelf, one hundred fathoms deep, generously extends all around Fogo Island. Until recently the fishing grounds off Fogo Island were ideal for fishers pursuing migratory salmon and cod in the summer, and cod in the fall.[2] Today some 3500 inhabitants live in eleven small communities all around the coastline of the island.

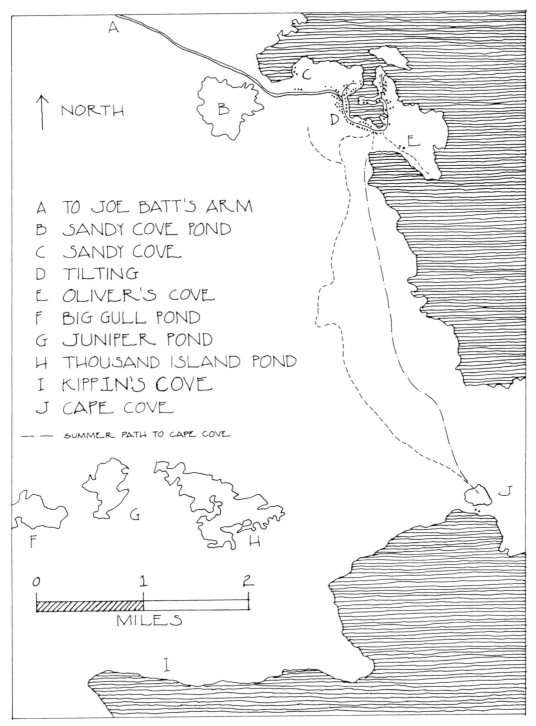

A TO JOE BATT'S ARM
B SANDY COVE POND
C SANDY COVE
D TILTING
E OLIVER'S COVE
F BIG GULL POND
G JUNIPER POND
H THOUSAND ISLAND POND
I KIPPIN'S COVE
J CAPE COVE

— · — SUMMER PATH TO CAPE COVE

NORTH

0   1   2
MILES

Map of the Tilting region, showing paths to Cape Cove

It is a hard place to live and to make a living, yet the people there have endured.

"Fogo" comes from the Portuguese "fuego" for fire. One nineteenth-century visitor described the island as, "extremely rugged and barren. It is nearly all bare rocks with scarcely a bush anywhere." In his eyes the landscape seemed to have "been swept clean by fire, and was probably in that condition when first discovered, hence the old navigator's name Fuego or Fire Island."[3]

It was first visited by fishers in the sixteenth century, but permanent European settlement did not begin until the eighteenth century. Fogo Island was regularly visited by the Beothucks when the first Europeans arrived, but contact between these groups was not congenial. By the end of the eighteenth century, English merchants had established trading premises, and the local fishers worked in extended-family fishing crews within a barter system that remained in force for more than a century.

The population remained stable for many years, spread out in small outports along the shoreline. In 1901 there were 3704 residents in the wonderfully named outports of Island Harbour, Deep Bay, Fogo, Shoal Bay, Barr'd Islands, Joe Batt's Arm, Tilting, Seldom-Come-By, Little Seldom, and Stag Harbour. These outports are still alive today. In addition, there were more remote settlements that have since disappeared, such as Payne's Harbour, Black Head Cove, Lion's Den, Wild Cove, Cape Cove, Indian Islands, and Little Fogo Islands.[4] In the late 1960s, the government of Newfoundland coerced and sometimes forced people in smaller and more remote communities to resettle in larger communities that were thought to be more accessible and better for long-term economic development. Fogo Island was one area targeted for resettlement. Tilting resident Ted Burke told me about government-sponsored resettlement from Cape Cove to Tilting.[5]

> Oh, yes—it should never be. 'Twasn't enough people left to
> keep a school, so the government got after them, so they all
> shift. We kept our place—house, stable, and stores—we

could go back in the summer—but the government wouldn't allow us to stay by yourself in the winter. So I bought this. We could still go back when you like, 'cause we never even brought the fork and knife out of it—we left it all down there—the whole lot. When we come up here, we fitted it right out 'cause it was a new home to us—we started buying kettles and pans and knives and forks and plates and everything. If we wanted to come up for a night in the harbor all we had to do is tackle the horse and come on—I had me stable there to put her in, I had me grass, I had the stage, had the house. And when we'd be coming up, we'd take three pails with us—and when we'd get to Long Pond we'd fill them with water—now we had a sleigh then, put the water on—come up here, we had our water.[6]

Yet, because of an intense effort on the part of Fogo Island inhabitants, most of the communities remained. Inspired by Memorial University of Newfoundland's Extension Service, residents living in isolated outports were united through an innovative, experimental process of community development based on the communicative possibilities of film. Extension service fieldworkers made documentary films in each community, and these were later used to show the residents of Fogo Island that they had common concerns. This process later became internationally known as the "Fogo Process."[7] From this movement the Fogo Island Cooperative Society was formed in 1967; FICS is still a thriving organization today. Although Fogo Island has lost about one-third of its population in the past ten years (from about 5000 down to 3500, the population of a hundred years ago), many residents still resist the temptation to relocate to what outsiders might believe are more comfortable and convenient centers elsewhere in Newfoundland or in Canada.

From the ferry terminal at Stag Harbour, the drive to Tilting is about forty-five minutes to the opposite end of Fogo Island, past the communities of Seldom-Come-By, Little Seldom, Shoal Bay, Barr'd Islands, and Joe Batt's Arm. After you pass Joe Batt's Arm, Tilting is five miles away at the end of the road, literally on the edge of the continent. If you want to proceed further, you have to go by boat: east to The Funks, now a bird sanctuary and once the home of the Great Auk,[8] or north to Little Fogo Islands, a small archipelago of islands about five miles off the coast, often visible from Tilting.

Coming down the hill to Tilting's Sandy Cove beach, on a clear day you can see all the way from Greene's Point on the eastern side of Tilting's harbor to The Cape, the site of the now-abandoned community of Cape Cove, about an hour and a half to the south by footpath. This is a windswept landscape of sea, rock, grassy meadows, marshes, bogs, ponds, woods, and sub-arctic flora and fauna. Inland you may occasionally see a wild herd of caribou. In mid-summer sightings of whales, icebergs, and large sea birds like gannets are common. Although rare, there have been encounters with polar bears that float down from Labrador on stray pans of ice.

Sandy Cove has the only large, sandy beach on Fogo Island, and it is a site with much history. On June 13, 1809, at a site now known as Turpin's Rock, Michael Turpin, a resident of Tilting, was killed by the Beothucks.[9] Sandy Cove once contained a small enclave of houses, outbuildings, gardens, and fishing stages, but only one house, a stable, and a root cellar remain today. The house and root cellar have recently been restored, retaining all their original features. At one time there were ten houses in Sandy Cove, and the houses and outbuildings were enclosed by one fence. This fence kept farm animals from grazing in the kitchen gardens and hay gardens around the houses.

During World War II Sandy Cove was also the home of the 185th United States Army Air Warning Squadron.[10] This base had bunkhouses, a cookhouse with a movie theater, a warehouse, and a hospital.[11] Residents from Tilting worked on the base, and they were pleased with the presence of the Americans, who would often visit people in Tilting. Some of the friendships between military personnel

A water hoop used for carrying water buckets (photo courtesy Clara Byrne)

U.S. Army servicemen on the military base at Sandy Cove during World War II (photo courtesy Clara Byrne)

and residents of Tilting endure to this day.[12] The base's radar building was located to the east of Sandy Cove at the top of Bunker Hill, site of the first Ground Radar Warning Station in the North Atlantic. No structures from the base remain in Sandy Cove, but after the base was dismantled, a few buildings were relocated to Tilting.[13] Some of the base's furniture and building components, like lumber and windows, were eventually recycled in many of Tilting's houses and outbuildings.

After you pass Sandy Cove and Bunker Hill, you will see your first close-up view of Tilting. Small, brightly painted houses and outbuildings surround the harbor in what at first appears to be a random pattern. These buildings, traditionally painted in the same manner as small wooden boats with many layers of shiny, brightly colored oil-base paint, perch precariously on their stiltlike foundations, making only tentative contact with the irregular terrain. Despite the appearance of an informal settlement pattern, this is a formal architecture of resistance, a cultural statement that challenges the forces of nature and decay. Yet, it is a fragile architecture that ultimately acknowledges that circumstances change, families get larger and then smaller, people move around or they move away, but life still goes on. Tilting's landscape has the character of a collage of elements that at times appears to have come from the drawings of a child, with no attempt to smooth abrupt connections and juxtapositions.

Settlement in Tilting began in the early eighteenth century, first by the French, later, for a short period, by a small contingent of English settlers,[14] followed by Irish settlers. There is some evidence of French occupation on the east side of the harbor near Greene's Point, where regularly placed small stones have been discovered under the sods. These are similar to the "graves" still found today on the French island of St. Pierre and Miquelon, locally known as "old Frenchman's flakes."[15]

Tilting owes its existence to the inshore cod fishery. James Candow has written about the conditions that led to nineteenth-century fishing communities like Tilting: "By the mid eighteenth century certain identifiable communities or 'regional centers' had begun to emerge. Merchants or their agents based in these centers began to devote more attention to trade, supplying the inhabitants with salt, fishing gear, basic foodstuffs, clothing, and domestic articles, and collecting their fish or other produce as payment. The common denominators among these regional centers tended to be good proximity to fishing grounds, a sheltered harbor with ample space for shore facilities, an abundant water supply, and access to other resources such as fur-bearing animals, salmon, and, increasingly, seals."[16]

Tilting was not just a fishing station, however. Irish immigrants first started to farm there in the early nineteenth century, and today Tilting is populated mainly by their descendants. According to Professor John Mannion, the first Irish settler in Tilting was Thomas Burke in 1752, born in Dungarvan in 1722.[17] As Michael Coady has written, "Thomas Burke began a dynasty which was uncommonly literate and literary in terms of 'outport' people struggling in a harsh environment. Some of the Burkes wrote journals and diaries; they built and skippered schooners (the Daniel O'Connell, the St. Declan) which took cargoes of fish far to the south and went north 'to the ice' (the seal fishery) in winter."[18]

Above: Ed Healey's house viewed from "The Bottom of the Pond," with a fishing stage and row punt
Below: The linear placement of houses on Greene's Point, with all houses facing the harbor

According to one source, Tilting got its name "because it was a place where fishermen used to tilt, that is, to head, split, and salt their fish. They used to erect small huts or camps of boughs, rinds, etc. while occupied in the tilting of the fish." Another source did not think the name Tilting "applied directly to the operation on the fish, but to the mode of living while so occupied."[19] Tilts were temporary wooden structures, constructed with vertical log walls and log roofs covered by birch rinds and sods, often built by migratory fishers before permanent settlements were established. The spelling of the community's name was officially changed from "Tilton" to "Tilting" in 1905 by the Committee on the Nomenclature of Newfoundland. "Tilting" was the original name of the settlement, and "Tilton" was a late-nineteenth-century corruption of this name. In order to avoid confusion with another community of the same name near Harbour Grace, Conception Bay,[20] the name was changed back to "Tilting."

Newfoundlanders voted to join Canada in 1949 in a referendum known as Confederation.[21] In pre-Confederation Tilting, people were allegiant to Ireland, not to Newfoundland. Also, many Tilting residents had relatives in the Boston area, locally called "The Boston States." During hard times in Tilting in the early twentieth century, some residents left to go to work in Boston. According to resident Jim McGrath, you can still hear different dialects in the harbor. Visitors from Ireland can tell where people came from in the old country, such as the Broders (from Waterford), the McGraths (from Cork), and the Greenes (from Carrick on Suir).

Modern conveniences came late to Tilting. Telegraphy service became available during World War I, and the first radios in Tilting date from the 1930s. Car ownership did not start until 1950, when Father Joseph M. O'Brien purchased a 1950 Chevrolet.[22] The first telephone came with the first public electricity service in the early 1960s, but some residents were resistant to the idea. Previously, a few families operated their own electricity generators.[23] Television arrived in Tilting at about the same time. Before the roads and ferry service to Fogo Island improved, mail would come once a week by coastal boat, which took one week to come from St. John's. Regular ferry service to Fogo Island did not start until 1962. Fergus Burke was the first person to drive from Fogo Island to St. John's in 1962. He made the trip on unpaved roads in a used 1959 Vauxhall, and it took twelve hours, quite

MARTIN GREENE ON AUTOMOBILES:
All hands wants a car now. The young fellow, he can't go out courtin' in the night—he wants a car—take out his girl, don't he? But when we were at it, you had to walk to see her. I don't know what you're going to think of me!

Father Joseph M. O'Brien's 1950 Chevrolet, parked in front of the church on the occasion of the bishop's visit to the parish (photo circa 1950 by Father J. M. O'Brien, courtesy Clara Byrne)

TED BURKE ON MODERNITY: In the fifties, 'twas fourteen families in Cape [Cove]—we were the only one that had a radio at that time—a Silvertone radio. After that, then everyone started getting them.

a speed record in those days.[24] The main roads to Fogo Island were not paved until the early 1990s.

In Tilting winter is long, and the fishing and farming season is short. The state of the weather is an important daily topic of conversation, and one's ability to cope with the weather remains to this day a prerequisite for survival. Before there were weather forecasts, people constantly searched for signs to monitor and predict the weather: the pattern and color of the sky, animals sheltering in the lun of a hill, or even the sound of a house. Annie Foley told me that when she lived in Sandy Cove, if her front door rattled, then it was too windy for the men to go out fishing.

Ted Burke taught me about Tilting's weather patterns. In June it is typically cold with variable winds. There is always a storm at the end of June, known as Peter and Paul. The best weather is in July and August, with prevailing southwesterly winds. In September it starts to cool down, and November is the start of winter. "I minds one winter we had to bar in all the cattle around the tenth of November." Slob weather comes in around New Year's, "northern slob we calls it," from the tenth of January until the end of the month. This means high northwesterly and northeasterly winds and cold temperatures before the ice comes in. After the end of January, more moderate weather can be expected. The winds die down, and there is more sun. The sea ice starts to pack into the harbor in February. From April to mid-May there is heavy, packed ice and rain, drizzle, and fog. By mid-May the ice on The Pond has typically melted, however, in some years it is so thick at the end of April that it can support slide hauling (harvesting wood by using a horse and slide). Sometimes the breakup of the ice also

TED BURKE ON THE WEATHER: I used to hear the old people saying, "Whatever the third day of the month is, that's the way that month will go out." I'm after tellin' people way older than myself about that, and they're after takin' notice. Here's another saying, "If you goes out the night of the full moon, if that star is only a short distance away from that moon, well you're going to get a civil month. But if that star is as far as from here to John Hurley's house, you can look out for the wind." That's what the old fellows used to say.

Out on the water, you'll always have a work up sky before you gets a storm. Real old dark clouds is on the sky—and perhaps if you're going to get a northeast wind, you'll see it way up over the islands. The old fellows, you know, they were pretty keen. The year the dogberries is plenty, it's going to be a mild winter. Now, I'm after hearing several different yarns about that. We were in Seldom one time with the mail. And the fellow that run the Post Office, he had a garden. Full of dogberries—so that was in December—and the dogberries was just like grapes on the tree then. So I said to the old man there, "What's that a sign of?" And he said, "Boy, that's the sign of a mild winter." And so it was. But anyways, I'm after hearing people saying, "When the dogberries stands on the trees, there's going to be lots of snow"—since the birds can pick off the dogberries off the trees. Same way in the fall of the year. If you sees the worms crossing the roads, it's going to be a mild winter. Say tomorrow, if the wind was southern, we'd all know if we're going to get rain. You'd know by the feel of the wind, you see. Wind would be right soft.

Greene's Point in winter, with ice covering The Harbour at the end of February

brought unforeseen benefits. One spring, after the ice melted, Fred Kinsella found Nick Lane's false teeth in the harbor. He had lost them in the ice and snow covering the harbor the year before, at the start of the winter.

In winter Tilting's landscape is transformed by ice. The only view of the sea and open water is a distant view, beyond the harbor. The Pond gradually freezes over, and in severe winters even the outer harbor is covered with ice. This transforms the community for pedestrians, turning a twenty-minute walk from a peninsula known as The Rock to St. Patrick's Church into a less-than-five-minute walk.

Until the late nineteenth century, families would sometimes move from Tilting to the more sheltered communities deep in Notre Dame Bay, like Boyd's Cove and Norris Arm, for the winter. Later, even when most families remained year round in Tilting, the men would often have to leave Fogo Island for months at a time without their families to supplement their fishing income by working in "the lumber woods"—there was no paid work during the winter on the island. Before the fisherman's cooperative, breaking even in one's account with the fish merchant was all that could be expected. Families experienced hard times when the fishery failed and during economic depressions.

The second church of St. Patrick's Parish (demolished in 1967) and the old Parish House (destroyed by fire in 1988) (photo by Father Edward Joseph O'Brien, shortly after the buildings were constructed, courtesy Newfoundland's Provincial Archives)

As was typical in the region, Catholics in Tilting were in regular contact for trade with Protestants in different communities on Fogo Island, but prejudices once prohibited common schools and marriage. These prejudices eventually diminished, and the present generation of senior citizens who regularly traveled outside the community were made to feel at home in almost every outport they happened to visit on Fogo Island and along the coast. Ted Burke told me about his regular visits to twenty-nine communities in Notre Dame Bay by boat when he worked for the post office, and about visiting between the communities of Seldom-Come-By and Cape Cove (closely affiliated with Tilting), on the southern shore of Fogo Island. "It's just the same as if you went into your own home—I can visit from Man O' War Cove to Lumsden—I can go into every house."

When I started my fieldwork in Tilting in 1987, I received a warm welcome in the community, but not without some perplexed reactions about my intentions. People could not understand why I was interested in old houses, locally made furniture, tools, boats, and gardens, since at the time the general feeling was that these things no longer had any

TED BURKE ON VISITING: Oh, yes, we got a lot of strangers [visitors to Cape Cove]—desperate lot of Seldom people—They says, "When we went to Cape Cove we're going home." Same thing applied to us, when we'd go to Seldom, if we were caught up there in a storm, we were going home—from point to point, from Button's Point to Burnt Point—'twas all our home, just the same as they'd come in your own home. We're all the one, and that's the way we wanted to be. But, there was a lot of difference in me grandfather's day. If he had a son going out with a Church of England girl, he'd be killed, right off the bat. Now that was foolishness, what? How could they make friends?

value. Despite its geographical isolation, by 1987 Tilting's residents were well aware of modern house construction techniques, and many people hoped to build new houses as soon as possible. Tilting's council was eager to modernize its infrastructure—to improve the roads and to provide a year-round water supply and a sewer system. Perhaps not realizing it at the time, the council was also making new regulations that, if enforced, could eventually change Tilting from a working farm into a residential community.[25]

I knew I had found a dynamic and unique place to do my fieldwork, a place that was in transition between the old and the new. I saw an old house for sale with an ideal view of the harbor, and shortly after purchased it. This house, Harold Dwyer's house, is a typical center hall–plan, two-story house built by his grandfather Gerald Dwyer in 1888. I never met Harold, who died just a few years before I arrived in Tilting, but his younger brother Pearce became my good friend. Pearce told me that Harold was well known as a sociable storyteller with a wonderful sense of humor, and that his house was an important destination for daily visiting in that part of the harbor. When my family moved into the house, it was just as Harold left it—with some of the original furniture made by his father and grandfather, and even his books, pictures, and dishes.

Over the course of the next year, I continued my fieldwork and made repairs to the house. I am sure I was not nearly as entertaining as Harold, but I still had many visitors. Terry Burke, Ned Cluett, and Mike Mahoney would regularly visit and tell me stories about the neighborhood, our house, and about Harold. Sometimes it seemed like

Quilt outside Ted and Agnes Burke's Gannet Head premises in Tilting

all I did was repair the house. At other times, I felt I was just living in Tilting, not really conscious of my research. I was gradually drawn into the life of the community, helping with small projects like the renovation of the Parish Club, assisting residents with their questions on house repairs and renovations, and occasionally participating in work activities like fishing in summer and hauling wood on the slide paths in winter.

Getting to know a community takes time. More than a year passed before I could feel Tilting's unique Irish heritage. I learned that Tilting was one of the only Irish Catholic communities on the northeast coast of Newfoundland, and that it had a proud tradition of educational excellence, producing many fine teachers, nurses, doctors, and other professionals. Tilting even had an active organization of expatriates in St. John's (Tilting Expatriates Association, or TEA) that met regularly for special events and produced a newsletter and handsome journal (*The Tilting Expatriate*) with articles about Tilting's customs and history. Slowly I was able to find out about Tilting's families, lifestyle, and the structures in which people lived and worked.

I have tried to keep the flow and pace of the interviews in this book as close as possible to the original, but it may help if you imagine their settings as you read them. A common background for many of the conversations was the evening light. While interviewing people in late afternoon, it often became too dark for me to see my notes. I would wait for someone to turn on the lights, but usually this did not happen until the room was nearly dark. The first few times this occurred, I became concerned, not wanting to interrupt the mood, but at the same time unable to write and forced to rely on my tape recorder. I gradually realized people in Tilting have an appreciation for the changing evening light, corresponding with a daily time to pause and reflect on the day's events. On a visit to Ben and Annie Foley's house, we started to chat in dim light and ended in near darkness. We sat in the dark for at least an hour, and this helped to focus the conversation. In the background there was the sound of Annie's rocking chair and the kettle simmering on the stove. In both summer and winter, evenings are often calm in Tilting, and the evening sky is dramatic.

This recollection of evening light reminds me of one of my mid-winter visits to Martin Greene's house. A young woman knocked on Martin's door in the mid-1980s to ask if he wanted to subscribe to cable television. Martin declined, since he did not have electricity in his house. When I would visit Martin to interview him on winter evenings, I would have to feel my way through the dark to find him in his back kitchen. Often, he would be sitting in the shadows next to his wood stove. Fortunately, I was able to use my tape recorder for interviews with Martin instead of relying on my notebook.

Dan Greene knows the land and sea around Tilting and told me about the history of place names, trap berths, slide paths, gardens,

FRANK MAHONEY ON VISITING OTHER COMMUNITIES:
Fogo Island is the only place now that you can go in and everyone is a friend. I can go up to Joe Batt's Arm and I can leave Brown's Point and go right down to the fish plant and I can speak to every man that's up there, because I knocked around with them.

Ted Burke demonstrating a scaffold brace

Harold McGrath on the new bridge he built around his house

Ben Foley and his son Gus in front of their "double store," a small store used for general storage

My children with playmates in the McGrath neighborhood in 1994. Top row (left to right): Hannah Mellin, Kenneth Burke, Holly Foley, Jill McGrath, Julia Mellin. Bottom row (left to right): Mary Claire McGrath, Melissa Foley.

Stella Burke and Gerard McGrath on the bridge leading to the back door of Gerard's house

Jim Greene in the early 1990s
(photo courtesy Patricia Greene)

houses, and outbuildings in remarkable detail. He can also teach you
how to do just about any work in Tilting, like fishing, curing fish and
hay, constructing buildings, and harvesting wood. He generously spent
much time with me, demonstrating many of these traditional practices
right on his own premises that are always impeccably maintained.
For the interviews, we would usually sit in his large back kitchen, but
many of the tape recordings were made while Dan and I walked around
his property so he could show me things while we talked.

Interviews with Jim Greene took place in his kitchen, with occasional walks around his premises. He was never shy about his positions
on recent developments in Tilting that he felt were eroding the way of
life he cherished. He had no time for those who would make you take off
your boots when you enter a house, incarcerate grazing animals, chase
caribou and destroy young trees with snowmobiles and ATVs, neglect
their vegetable gardens, and overfish capelin and cod. In late-1960s
black-and-white National Film Board films, you can see Jim as a younger
man, a formidable foe of resettlement and other perceived injustices
of the time on Fogo Island.[26]

Ted Burke's descriptions of life in Cape Cove and Tilting were
highly detailed, and he always used storytelling to convey morals. In
this sense, he was a good teacher. Through Ted, it became obvious how
important storytelling was in the past for oral history and continuity

ANNIE FOLEY ON ST. PATRICK'S DAY:
At one time they used to parade right around the harbor. Go right over on Greene's Point and turn and come right back again—and come to the church. Uncle Ambrose used to bring the big flag from Sandy Cove. That night they'd have a big party in the hall.

between generations. When I read the transcripts of our interview sessions, in my mind I hear the sound of his deep voice—musical, calm, and assured, with numerous sustained pauses heightening the drama of his stories.

Visiting the kitchens of Rose Burke, Dorothy Burke, Gertrude Dwyer, Edith Reardon, Alice Greene, Christine Broders, Agnes Foley, Margaret Broaders, Stella Burke, and many other remarkable women taught me much about daily life and work in Tilting. When I visit Tilting now, I do not get to visit people as often as I used to. But Gladys McGrath always welcomes my family and makes us feel we are truly at home. Her kitchen is the cognitive center of a large part of the McGrath neighborhood, where children, friends, and relatives visit in a constant flow during the day. Many of my interviews took place in this kitchen, often with more than one person in attendance. Cups of tea, laughter, and a genuine sense of community always accompanied these sessions. This kitchen is my touchstone, a place I know I can always visit to slow the passage of time.

Above: Annie Foley
Opposite: Gladys McGrath and her son Neil in their back kitchen

Today there's nothing, only rock and gravel wherever you look. When I first came out here, there was a nice lot of grassy land, especially in the summer time when everything turned green and looked lovely. There's not a place to sit down now—there were so many landmarks, like rocks—there was a rock out here called Tag Rock. All hands used to sit down on that. And there was another place up there, the Lane's Rocks, where Mr. Gilbert lives. Men would be sitting up there—and then there was another rock down the end of the lane, they used to call it the Spell Rock—and that was a gallery for people. Everything is destroyed. Everything's gone. The men used to go up there: they could see out over the water, see if they could see their family coming in. Another thing I never sees now is the sheep's path. My God, in Sandy Cove you'd follow their paths right down along. You'd have about fifty or sixty sheep together and they'd all go the one way and they'd wear the ground right down and here's the hay growing right up on each side of this, just like a street—so far apart—right narrow, and go right on down, over the hill. We often traveled them for hours—follow the sheep's path. Take you right out to the harbor where they come in over the side of Bunker Hill.

CHAPTER 1

RUGGED LANDSCAPE, STRONG PEOPLE, FRAGILE ARCHITECTURE

-- -- -- -- -- -- -- -- -- --

*T*ILTING IS LOCATED ON ONE of the most rugged and
exposed parts of the northeastern coast of Fogo Island. James P.
Howley described the area in 1871: "This portion of our coast off the
N.E. of Fogo Island is one of the very worst and most dangerous.
Besides the celebrated Barracks, numerous other Islands and Island
rocks strew the ocean for many miles. Many a fine sealing vessel or
Labradorman had come to grief on those awful rocks and shoals."[1]
There are no trees to offer shelter from winds and storms, and there is
only one small island, Pigeon Island, to buffer heavy seas. Without
Pigeon Island, Tilting's harbor would be impossible to navigate. Even
with Pigeon Island, navigation can be difficult in stormy weather.
Greene's Point provides the main protection from the open sea to the
east of the harbor, but the older residents remember brutal storms and
tidal waves when the sea would sometimes run over this land. In 1935
a tremendous storm destroyed all the Greene's fishing stages and
convinced some of them it was time to move to safer ground elsewhere
in the community.

Tilting's harbor has an outer area called "The Harbour" and an
inner area called "The Pond," which is partly separated from the harbor
by a peninsula called "The Rock." The Rock used to be an island, but
it is now connected to the shore by a causeway. Before travel by road
replaced travel by sea, all houses faced the waterfront, turning it into a
stage. "The first thing a man wanted to do in the morning when he
opened his eyes was to look at the harbor."[2] The facades of the houses
were oriented toward the arrival of visitors. Windows were the eyes
of the house, extending a formal welcome at all times, whether or not
anyone was at home. Today, since travel by road is the main mode of
travel, new houses are built with the front of the house facing the road.
Some of the older houses that originally faced the harbor were later
turned on their foundations to face the road.

Tilting's houses cluster around the shoreline of The Harbour and
The Pond, and they are sited to conserve the land available for gardens

Fishing stages on Greene's Point: Mike Greene's stage (left) and Dan Greene's stage (right)

Boys "rafting" on The Pond: (left to right) David, Wade, and Dale Dwyer

according to the mediaeval infield and outfield garden practices once used in Ireland. This settlement pattern is one of the most interesting aspects of Tilting's cultural landscape because it is so different from the fenced-in, individually owned farms typical of most of the North American landscape. In Tilting vegetables grown in the infield gardens are usually for summer and fall consumption, and vegetables grown in remote outfield gardens are for the winter vegetable supply. The remote gardens are clustered with the gardens of neighbors at The Farm in Sandy Cove or in Oliver's Cove, where sea kelp is readily available for fertilizer. It takes about fifteen or twenty minutes to walk to these gardens from Tilting. Although most of Tilting's activity is centered around the harbor, the physical territory of the community is greatly extended in winter by slide paths for hauling wood and in summer by trap berths for fishing.

The Rock Bridge before a causeway was constructed for vehicular access to The Rock (photo courtesy Clara Byrne)

Throughout the community, you see delicate picket fences made from the narrow trunks of fir and spruce trees hauled to Tilting from the forests on the south coast of Fogo Island. There are no trees in Tilting, which heightens the awareness of its architecture. The coastal landscape has a low, horizontal inflection, a sense of propinquity, of being close to the sea. There are no tall structures and no dramatic hills. The coastline is rocky, and there is a powerful visual connection between the rock and the sea. Tilting's connection with the sea is evident everywhere in the form of fishing stages. These extensive, amphibious structures, made with local timber, are distributed all around the shoreline of the harbor.[3] They provide access to deeper water for mooring small boats. In the summer, around the harbor you can still see many locally made traditional wooden boats like row punts and trap skiffs.

Before paved roads were constructed for cars, Tilting's roads were more like narrow lanes, lined on both sides by picket fences. Small wooden bridges spanned natural drainage channels and linked small islands like Kelly's Island and The Rock. In recent years some of the prominent rock landmarks, such as "The Rock in the Garden" next to Doreen and Pearce Dwyer's house, have been removed where it was thought they were either too close to the road or too dangerous for children's play. Tilting's older residents lament the demise of "the old Tilting" when recalling the narrow lanes and landmarks that were once part of the landscape, gradually dug out to make way for new house foundations or water and sewer pipes.

The builders of older houses in Tilting did not try to change the topography of the land, and so often built on uneven ground. This is

Mike, Dan, and Gerard Greene's fishing stages (from left to right) on Greene's Point

ANNIE FOLEY ON FENCES: That was the reason it was fenced in. Everybody in the harbor had cows, and horses, and sheep, and the place was teeming with animals. If you had it all open like it is now, the animals would be all in. The nicest place on Fogo Island in the summer time Sandy Cove was.

The road to Oliver's Cove

A picket fence behind Dan Greene's premises

The last days of freedom for Fogo Island's Newfoundland ponies, grazing in Sandy Cove. Tilting's municipal council passed bylaws restricting open grazing of animals a year after this photograph was taken.

not acceptable for today's new house construction, since a major part of the image of a new house is a large, level, ornamental front lawn. The front lawn of the new house also heightens the separation between public and private areas around the dwelling. These separations were not so evident in the past. Despite these changes, the overall historical character of the community is still evident, with the old coexisting with the new.

Today the grass grows long and wild in Tilting, but it was not always that way. Animal husbandry based on the old, Irish homeland system of open field grazing or commonage (communal grazing)[4] was once the style in Tilting. In the nineteenth and early twentieth centuries, Tilting's residents kept hundreds of sheep and many cows, goats, pigs, and chickens. Fences were used to keep animals out of gardens and off the top of root cellars, rather than to keep them penned in. On my first trip to Tilting, I had to stop my car to wait for a large herd of roaming horses to cross the road. I was very fortunate to see Tilting's landscape before restrictions were placed on open field grazing of animals in the late 1980s. Some Tilting residents decided they no longer wanted to live on a farm and complained that the animals were ruining their front yards, so the town council passed a bylaw against roaming animals. In the past, however, there was more tolerance of the presence of animals, and less interest in maintaining a formal front yard. People used to have a sense of humor about the animals. Not only did animals get into gardens, they sometimes got into houses. Fergus Burke told me about the cow that once went into a house and walked up the steps to the second floor. Apparently, they had a difficult time getting her downstairs and out of the house.

This change in animal husbandry from open to enclosed areas was not unique to Tilting. In Newfoundland today, all municipalities have to conform to regulations prohibiting open, unrestricted grazing by animals if they wish to obtain government support for infrastructure projects. This would seem to work against tourism and against the preservation of the unique characteristics of Newfoundland's cultural landscape. Before the bylaw all the casual, unfenced grass areas around houses and outbuildings were thoroughly manicured by the animals. The grass was thriving—intensely green and very short, and there were few nettles or weeds. It looked like gardeners had been employed on a full-time basis to maintain the grounds. The only tall grass was the grass in the fenced-in hay meadows.

Due to the lack of suitable fenced pastureland, the regulation prohibiting open grazing has created hardships for residents who keep

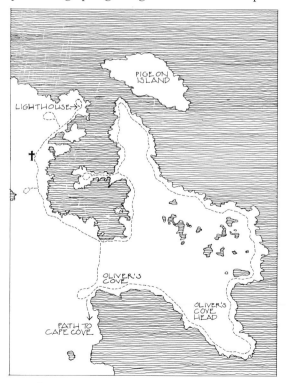

Map of the path for a walking tour of Tilting

The third church of St. Patrick's Parish (to the left, with the old Parish House and other houses in the neighborhood)

animals. My friend Cyril McGrath has resorted to grazing his sheep on Little Fogo Islands in the summer where they will not disturb anyone. Each spring Cyril gently ties their legs together and places them in his open motorboat for the five-mile trip to the islands. It is a curious sight to see twelve to fifteen sheep riding over the open sea in a motorboat.[5]

When you first enter Tilting, you arrive in the most public part of the harbor with the highest density of houses and outbuildings. At the main intersection of the road around the harbor stands the third church of St. Patrick's Parish constructed on this site, a modern building that now serves as an anguished reminder of the destruction of the second church by a newly arrived Irish priest who was determined to leave his mark on the North American landscape as soon as possible. St. Patrick's Parish was founded in 1835, and Tilting was always the head of the parish. Construction of the second church started in 1900, and the first mass to be celebrated there was the Christmas midnight mass of 1902. It was demolished in 1967.[6]

Next to the church once stood the old Parish House, later the Parish Club, destroyed by fire in 1988, and two schools, only one of which remains today as a youth recreation center. The last year children went to elementary school in Tilting was 1987. Across the road and up the lane was the old post office, a building with a special roof shape identifying its public function. Also found at this intersection was Burke's store, a false-fronted building typical of general stores found in many outport communities, similar in appearance to Hurley's old store. The old store was demolished, but Hurley's business still thrives in Tilting today. Walking to the edge of the road along the north shore of the harbor past Murray's Island and Kelly's Island, you reach the Lane house, the oldest house in Tilting, now a local museum for Tilting's historical artifacts. Past the Lane house and France's Cove,[7] you reach the site of the old wooden lighthouse on Sloan's Hill (also known as Lighthouse Hill). The lighthouse was constructed according to a standard, government-issued plan, and it had a small, enclosed stair for light-keeper access.[8] Backtracking a bit, you can make a slight detour behind the Lane house to Tilting's oldest cemetery. This cemetery is known as the old Irish cemetery, and it has headstones dating back to the 1790s.[9]

Retracing your steps to the church and proceeding on the main road around the harbor heading south, you pass through the McGrath and Foley neighborhoods, past many houses and outbuildings. Heading up Lane's Rocks, to your right is a lane leading to the Parish Hall, present home of the St. Patrick's Parish Club. St. Patrick's is one of the few parishes in North America that has its own pub. Looking to the east out to the harbor, you can see the small channel of water known as The Pond Tickle that runs between the main shoreline and The Rock

The old post office, a building with a special roof shape identifying its public function

Martin Hurley's old false-fronted store near Hurley's Cove. The Davis house was attached to the back of this building to increase the storage area.

Left: The Lane house
Right: The Parish Hall near the Lane's Rocks area of Tilting. The Parish Club is located in this building.

in the center of the harbor. Before cars became available, people made daily use of row punts to travel from one side of the harbor to the other for trips to school, mass, the post office, and two business establishments on The Rock.

After Lane's Hill you pass through the Lane and Broders neighborhoods, past prominent rock landmarks. On your right at the foot of a rocky cliff in an area known as The Gulch, you see old houses sheltered from prevailing southwesterly winds. Then you enter the Keefe (formerly O'Keefe) and Hurley neighborhoods, where you will find an unpaved road leading to Oliver's Cove. A long time ago, it was the custom to take a Sunday walk on this road to Oliver's Cove and Oliver's Cove Head.

After you go up the hill to Oliver's Cove, you will see an example of what Tilting must have looked like at one time, with picket fences defining the lanes, and well-maintained gardens and pastures. In July the meadows are covered with yellow and purple wildflowers, mostly buttercups and irises. Oliver's Cove's gardens are still intensively used, and there you will still find several root cellars and a hay house. The old style of potato, turnip, and cabbage beds are used in these gardens. Here the rich soil has been built up over many generations, fertilized with kelp and capelin from the beach. There were two houses in Oliver's Cove at one time, occupied by William and James Hurley's families, but there are no houses there today.

A typical gate in a picket fence in Oliver's Cove

If you want to walk to the abandoned community of Cape Cove, you pick up the footpath past the bridge by the beach in Oliver's Cove. Oliver's Cove is one of my favorite spots in Tilting. It has a small, well-protected beach with round beach stones, and its gardens are sheltered behind the beach in a protected valley. The bridge crosses a small stream that runs through the valley. In the summer months, Tilley, Albert Cluett's Newfoundland pony, is usually in a fenced pasture in the middle of the gardens. The last time I saw her (July 2001) she had just foaled in this garden a half hour before I arrived.

Walking along the north shore of Oliver's Cove to Oliver's Cove Head, you pass Potato Hole Point. In this location the early settlers in Tilting would store potatoes in shallow hillside excavations in the earthen banks by the gardens. After passing Hurley's Cove, Mik Keefe's Point, Copper Cove, Sweeney's Gulch, The Raggedy Nuddick, The Tickle of the Head, and The Rock of the Head, you arrive at Oliver's Cove Head. These curious and lyrical place names are typical of Tilting's cultural landscape. Every year in my conversations with Tilting's residents, I learn more of these place names. There are many place names

Left: Fenced gardens in Oliver's Cove showing the type of raised bedding used for planting potatoes and cabbage
Right: The old wooden lighthouse on Lighthouse Hill. This lighthouse had a small, winding stair for access to the light.

for paths, work areas, landforms, and landmarks. They function like an index that assists in the recollection of local history, people, and events.

The stretch of shoreline just traversed is a capelin spawning area. In July the presence of gannets, large, graceful sea birds that nest on The Funk Islands in summer, in Oliver's Cove signals the arrival of the capelin, small fish craved also by cod and whales. People line up on the rocky shore to fish for capelin using traditional cast nets. In capelin spawning season you can see whales in Oliver's Cove, sometimes breaching just a hundred feet offshore.

From Oliver's Cove Head you can proceed north to return to Tilting along the east coast trail where you will see the remains of abandoned remote gardens, with regularly spaced furrows of old potato beds visible under the sods. The last picket fences in this area disappeared in the late 1980s. This is a sea-scoured landscape of sculpted rock, small ponds, coves, bogs, and marshes. As this shoreline is very exposed, care must be taken to keep away from heavy breaking seas. You pass Tom Ryan's Gulch, Pummely Cove, Pummely Cove Point, Pummely Cove Pond, Middle Point, John Fowlow's Harbour, Careless Point Pond, Careless Point, The Goat House, The Big Lookout, The Little Lookout, and The Washing Ponds. True to their name, The Washing Ponds were once used for clothes washing by people living on the east side of the harbor. After these ponds you pass the rock landmark known as The Devil's Rocking Chair and then Bluff Head. At the northern tip of this trail, across from Pigeon Island, you arrive at Garrison Point. There is some speculation that this was the location of an old French Garrison in Tilting.[10]

From Garrison Point you walk along the eastern shore of the harbor past the houses and fishing stages on Greene's Point, through the Greene and Burke neighborhoods. Pausing at Dan Greene's for a while, you will see one of the best-maintained traditional premises in Newfoundland. Dan Greene's premises follow the typical linear layout for properties on Greene's Point. On the ocean side of the road (east side), the garden, stable, and root cellar are located on the same

Place names in Tilting

1. *Johnson's Pond*
2. *Black Rock*
3. *Black Rock Tickle*
4. *Bunker Hill*
5. *Backside*
6. *Lighthouse Hill*
7. *Morey's Point*
8. *France's Cove*
9. *Kelly's Island*
10. *Johnson's Bridge*
11. *The Old Cemetery*
12. *Johnson's Rock*
13. *Murray's Island*
14. *Church Lane*
15. *The Church*
16. *The Cemetery*
17. *Henan's Hill*
18. *Henan's Pond*
19. *The Pond Tickle Rocks*
20. *The Pond Tickle*
21. *Ter's Tickle*
22. *Uncle Ter's Island*
23. *Peter's Cove and John Haughton's Rock*
24. *Collybou, Hay's Point, and The Nap*
25. *Lane's Rocks*
26. *Broder's Height*
27. *The Gulch*
28. *Ambrose McGrath's Pond*
29. *Palmer's Marsh*
30. *Haughton's Woody Hill*
31. *The Gallows*
32. *Matthas's Height*
33. *Gannet Head*
34. *Hurley's Cove*
35. *Mill Pond*
36. *Nor'd Point*
37. *Maurice Lyon's Cove*
38. *South Point*
39. *Flat Point*
40. *Oliver's Cove Beach*
41. *Oliver's Cove Bridge*
42. *Potato Hole Point*
43. *Oliver's Cove*
44. *Oliver's Cove Height*
45. *Hurley's Cove*
46. *Mik Keefe's Point*
47. *Copper Cove*
48. *Sweeney's Gulch*
49. *The Raggedy Nuddick*
50. *Tickle of the Head*
51. *Rock of the Head*
52. *Oliver's Cove Head*
53. *Tom Ryan's Gulch*
54. *Pummely Cove*
55. *Pummely Cove Pond*
56. *Pummely Cove Point*
57. *Middle Point*
58. *John Fowlow's Harbour*
59. *Careless Point Pond*
60. *Careless Point*
61. *The Goat House*
62. *The Washing Ponds*
63. *The Big Lookout*
64. *The Little Lookout*
65. *Lar's Gulch*
66. *Herring Gulch*
67. *The Devil's Rocking Chair*
68. *The Baiting Pond*
69. *Bluff Head*
70. *Eastern Tickle*
71. *Eastern Point*
72. *The Cod Bag*
73. *Wing Point*
74. *Pigeon Island*
75. *Shallop Rock*
76. *Landing Cove*
77. *Western Point*
78. *Garrison Point*
79. *The Harbour*
80. *Greene's Point*
81. *The Little Harbour Rock*
82. *The Big Harbour Rock and Barnacle Pond*
83. *Bullock's Island and Coleman's Cove*
84. *Blubber Cove*
85. *Coleman's Lane*
86. *The Rock*
87. *Martin's Hill*
88. *The Rock in the Garden*
89. *Higgin's Height or Cluett's Height*
90. *Hurley's Island or Reardon's Island*
91. *Davis's Point*
92. *The Bottom of the Pond*
93. *The Pond*

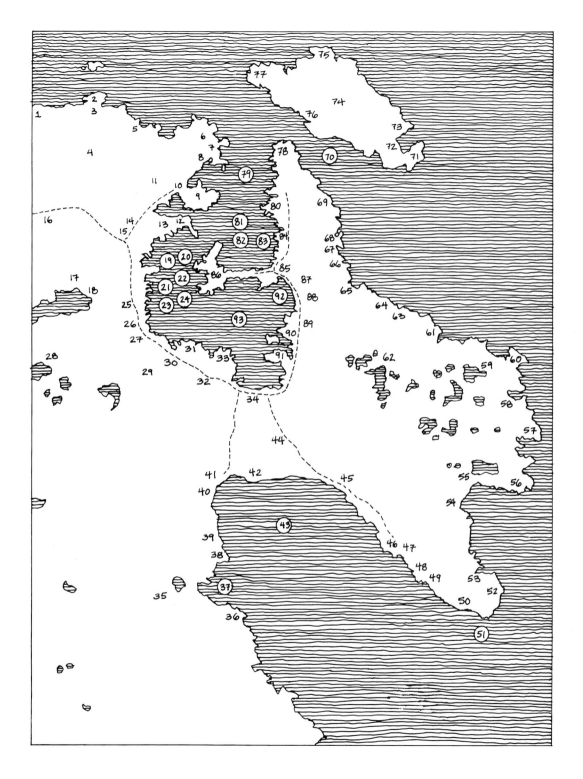

Left: Some of the Burke family's outbuildings on Greene's Point
Below: Houses and outbuildings on Greene's Point

GREENE'S
POINT

N

DAN & THERESA
GREENE

DOROTHY & LOUIS
BURKE

THE
HARBOUR

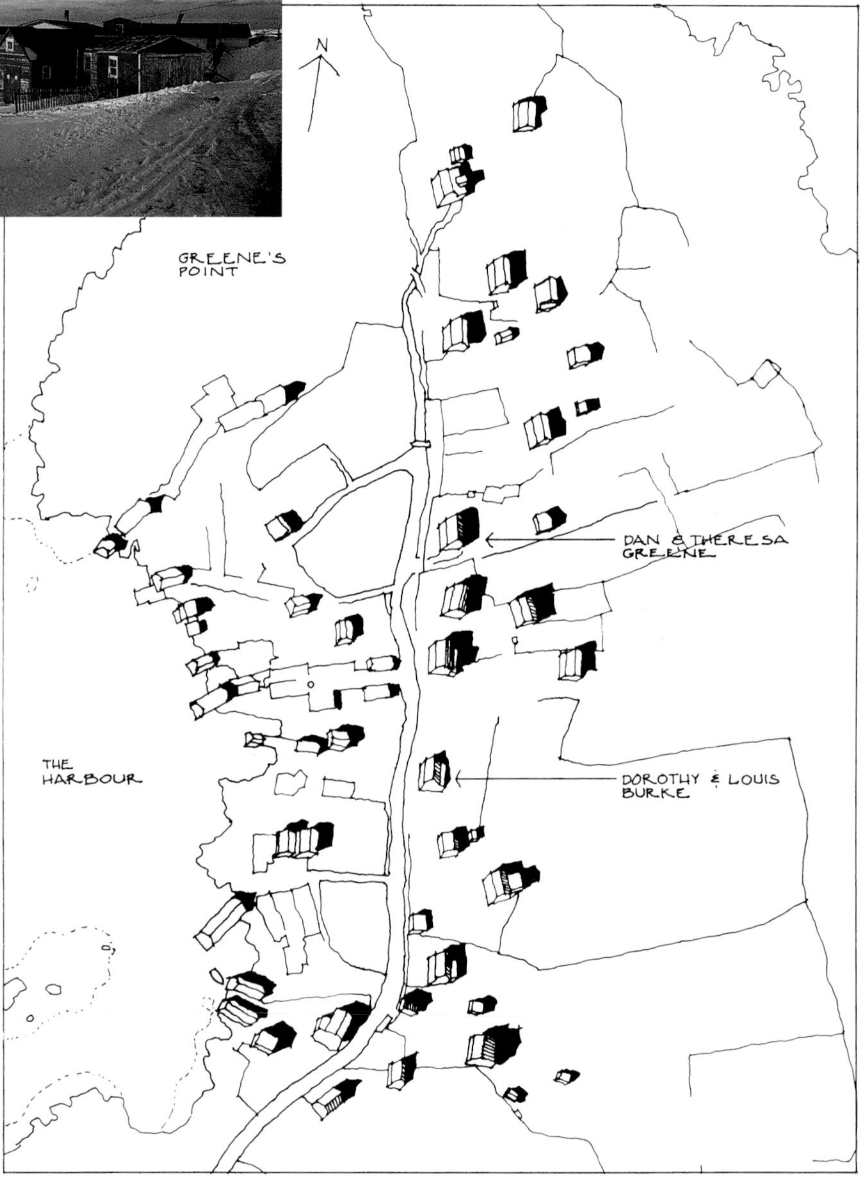

Above: The view over Dan Greene's front gate to his fishing premises across the road

Right: Dan Greene's premises on Greene's Point. On the ocean side of the road (the east side), the stable and root cellar are located in the same garden as the house. The twine store, stage, and flake are located on the harbor side of the road.

1. Ocean
2. Slide storage / path
3. Cellar
4. Cabbage house
5. Ned's potatoes
6. Stable / woodshed
7. Wood cutting
8. Wood storage
9. Chickens
10. Clothes drying
11. Well
12. House
13. Hay meadow
14. Location of former stable
15. Drying nets
16. Twine store
17. Flakes
18. Stage
19. Harbor

plot of land as the house. The twine store, flakes, and stage are located on the harbor side of the road directly opposite the house. Neighbors usually do not cross paths on Greene's Point except when walking down the road. An exception is the intersection of bridges leading to Dan Greene's and Gerard Greene's stages, where paths cross in midair on a raised bedding or flake.

After passing Blubber Cove, you come to a fork in the road. Turn right and you soon reach the site of the Albert Dwyer premises, a restored house, twine store, flake, and fishing stage open to the public. On calm days you can take the old row punt out for a cruise on The Pond. Proceeding further, you reach The Rock, presently the home of the Foleys, Cluetts, Kinsellas, Dwyers, and Bryans. The Kinsella premises, like Dan Greene's premises, are impeccably maintained. There you will see a unique group of attached outbuildings that, together with the fishing stage, form a protected work courtyard next to the house. In addition to houses, two public buildings are located on The Rock, the fire hall and the community stage. The fire hall was once a branch of the Fishermen's Protection Union Trading Company, but the original building was smaller and had a false front. The Rock was always the main site of Tilting's mercantile premises for the fishery and for bulk provisions. Before the co-op and the trading company arrived, the Bryan family operated the main mercantile premises.

Old fire hall, formerly the Fishermen's Protection Union
Trading Company store

The interior of the restored fishing stage on Albert Dwyer's premises. The stage floor or "bedding" is open to the water below.

A view of Blubber Cove from Coleman's Lane

Albert and Philomena Cluett's house on The Rock, formerly the Bryan's house

This was followed by a branch of Earle's, merchants with their main premises in the town of Fogo.

Returning to the main road and walking south, you pass houses owned by the Mahoneys, Dwyers, and Reardons. In this part of the harbor, water is shallow and extended fishing stages were required to reach deeper water. At The Bottom of the Pond, there is a sandy beach area where people used to dig for clams for bait at low tide. You pass Higgin's Height and Reardon's Island, the site of a recently restored fishing stage, flake, and twine store. After you pass Hurley's Cove, you once again reach the intersection with the road to Oliver's Cove. Returning to the church, you have completed this three-hour itinerary.

As you walk around the harbor, you see prominent rocks that are still used as unique gathering places for viewing harbor activities and socializing. These rocks have been used for many generations. Some are used by children (Kids Rock in The Gulch), some by adolescents (rock by Mike Keefe's), and others by retired fishermen (Lane's Rocks by Lawrence Broder's house and the rock next to Mark Foley's house). In addition to these locations, there were viewing gallery rocks by Walter Bryan's house on The Rock (known as The Nap, and used by Kinsellas, Foleys, and Dwyers), on Burke's Hill by Terry Burke's house (used by Greene's, Burkes, and Dwyers), and on Matthas's Height (used by Greenes, Cluetts, and Keefes). People would often gather in these locations on Sundays after mass or in the evening.[11]

Tilting's residents still live in extended-family neighborhoods identified by family names and by place names. The main family neighborhoods from east to west are the Greene, Burke, Sexton, Dwyer, Keefe, Broders, Lane, Foley, and McGrath neighborhoods. There are also smaller neighborhoods of Greenes, Mahoneys, Burkes, Dwyers, Broaders,[12] and Foleys.[13] Other families not identified here can be found within or adjacent to these neighborhoods. To the visitor, neighborhoods in Tilting have no obvious visual boundaries. The placement of houses and outbuildings in the McGrath family neighborhood and in several other similar neighborhoods resulted from the allotment of

Well, I'll tell you—they were Irishmen and they couldn't get handy enough to the water—It's a wonder they didn't build the house on that island out there in the middle of the pond.

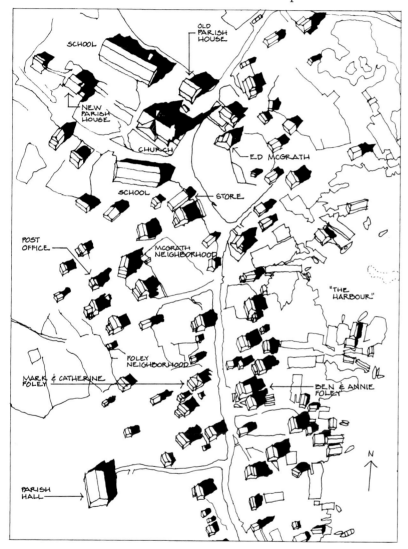

Left: The McGrath and Foley neighborhoods
Right: Cyril McGrath on his long-liner, shared with his brothers Leo, Frank, and Andrew

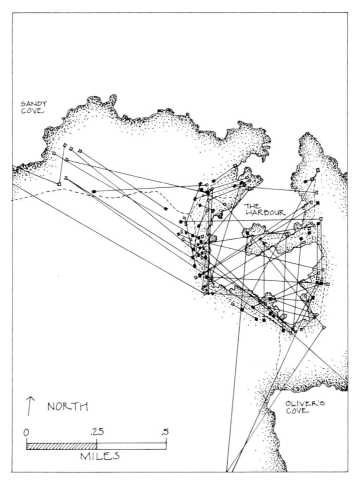

SANDY COVE

THE HARBOUR

OLIVER'S COVE

↑ NORTH

0   .25   .5

MILES

House launching in Tilting. Some houses were launched or moved two or three times, even to or from other communities.

land through inheritance and thus produced a mixed pattern.[14] Fergus Burke told me that his grandfather owned land that was subdivided and given to his sons. Typically, the old family home was inherited by the youngest son, but all sons got some land. They would either build a new house or buy one and "launch" it to their land (just as boats are launched, when houses were moved in Tilting, they were "launched").

The lack of rigid property boundaries reflects the extended family's cooperative approach to the fishery. Outbuildings located on the same plot of land as the house are the exception in the McGrath neighborhood. These outbuildings are generally single-purpose structures, such as stages, flakes, and twine stores on the harbor side of the road, and houses, stables, general stores, and cellars on the opposite

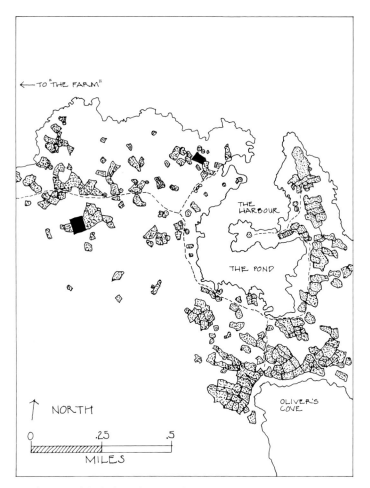

Gardens around the harbor and in Oliver's Cove. The old cemeteries are shaded in black.

side. Some outbuildings, such as those for the fishery, were often shared because brothers fished together. To reach their stages and twine stores on the harbor side of the road, the McGraths had to make their way down the paths past other McGrath houses, outbuildings, and gardens. They were always passing each other's buildings and houses in the course of their daily chores, ensuring that people were in daily contact. The location of outfield gardens also had this effect. Paths were crossed on the way to and from the gardens, and trust and cooperation were required to maintain fences, paths, and rights of way. The McGrath neighborhood has a mixed, clustered order in contrast to the Greene neighborhood on Greene's Point. There, the neighborhood order is linear and distinct. This, coupled with less dwelling density on Greene's

Newfoundland weather was wonderful variable and
the seasons were different—no two seasons alike.

Point and also the isolated location, contributes to a sense of greater
privacy in that part of the harbor.

Over time neighborhoods changed in area and subdivided, and
houses changed locations as families moved away from Tilting. The
practice of moving houses and outbuildings between communities,
between neighborhoods, and within neighborhoods further contributed
to a mixed pattern.[15] A mixed pattern, what Tilting's residents would
probably call a "tangle," also occurs between houses and gardens.[16]
Often the worst land was used for buildings and the best land was
reserved for gardens. Some families were fortunate to have a garden
near the house, but such land was limited and other gardens, often
located far from the house, were required.[17] Families living between
Kelly's Island and Lane's Rocks had their gardens in Sandy Cove, and
those between Lane's Rocks and Greene's Point had their gardens at
Oliver's Cove.

In Tilting the topography does not influence house form. The
house has autonomous value and its relation to its site is enigmatic.
The overall pattern of the facades of the houses facing the harbor is
further fragmented by the topography.[18] The link between houses and
outbuildings and their immediate surroundings is tenuous, as if they
could be moved at any time. The immediate site is nearly ignored in the
placement of the house, and houses are placed in gardens or on rocks
in what appears to be a casual manner. Houses rarely go beyond a
tentative acknowledgment of their site, such as fitting a foundation skirt
to the rocks, extending a porch with a bridge, or placing an ornamental
garden adjacent to the house.

Tilting's houses are only one component of a typical set of
essential small-scale structures owned by each family. If they could be
separated from other family's premises and combined in one location,
these structures would appear like a small village: the twine store, stage,
flakes, and fish store for the fishery; the stable, hay shed, milk house,
hen house, pig pound, root cellar, and cabbage house for agriculture

Foundation shores painted in different colors supporting the stores behind the Kinsella house on The Rock

Bernard Cluett's house on The Rock

Bridges from Albert and Philomena Cluett's house to their stable

Houses and outbuildings on The Rock

and animal husbandry; and also the carpentry shop, wood store, general store, coal house, outhouse, grub store, and garage. Finally, there are the outhouse, trap skiffs, row punts, wooden puncheons, slides, nets, lobster pots, large iron barking pots, stacked firewood, fences, and many locally made devices like killicks, barrows, and tools.

The community still follows a seasonal pattern of work: fishing and agriculture in the summer, harvesting, berry picking, and hay cutting in late summer and fall, and cutting and hauling firewood in the winter. There has also been a great revival of interest in agriculture and animal husbandry. Gardens and pastures, which had been deteriorating in the 1970s and 80s, are once again being maintained.

Mary Lane, wife of fisherman Nicolas Lane, described her typical day during the fishing season when she was first married. At six A.M.

she would rise and start cooking and washing. Twice a week she would make bread. Some mornings she would saw wood or pick berries. By nine or ten in the morning the men would be back from fishing. Before they had breakfast, they would wash out two or three tubs of fish and spread them on the flakes. After breakfast Mary would card or spin wool, or sew. Dinner was around two P.M., and after this the men would go back to fishing. Supper was at six P.M., and bed at eleven P.M. Mary did not mention other strenuous daily work that she had to do, of backbreaking hours spreading fish on the flake, tending gardens, making hay, and hunting cows.

For the fishers of Tilting, going to sea in small wooden boats was a daily act of courage. As Dan Greene described it to me, you had to row out and back under your own power. There were no life jackets, no reliable weather forecasts, no search and rescue agencies, and no ship-to-shore radios. A sudden change of weather could blow you out to sea.

Cod trap berths were located between Round Head to the west and the Fishing Gulch to the east. Fishermen used to put out their "marks" to claim their trap berths at midnight on the first of June, and a minimum distance of eighty fathoms between berths was the rule. Families were usually able to maintain the same berths from year to year, and family names were always associated with particular berths. Also, fishers from other communities on Fogo Island often came to the area around Tilting to fish. Fergus Burke remembers men fishing near Tilting from as far away as Carmanville and Bonavista Bay (St. Brendan's, Wesleyville). During the fishing season, the harbor was often full of schooners from other communities.

Before the federal government constructed the community stage (a central facility for unloading and processing fish), the best areas for settlement within the community were those with water deep enough for direct access by boat to the fishing stages. Areas like The Bottom of the Pond were less desirable, and the shallow water in these areas required the construction of long bridges to extend the stages to deeper water. The first area to be settled was on the west side of the harbor, and the less desirable, shallow water areas were settled by later arrivals like "sharemen" and "dieters" (sharemen received a share of the catch, and dieters received board and lodging in exchange for their work).

Tilting's fishers made their living by using their small wooden boats for the "inshore" fishery close to shore. There were good years and bad years, but no one could ever have imagined that one day the cod would disappear. From the mid-twentieth century on, large government- and company-owned draggers fished the cod stocks off Newfoundland's coast. Fishing many miles out at sea, these vessels were the mainstay of the "offshore" cod fishery. Overfishing by these vessels eventually caused both the inshore and offshore cod fishery to close, and many residents living in rural communities like Tilting had to leave Newfoundland to find work elsewhere. Dedicated fishers with a lifetime of experience and local knowledge of the sea and weather conditions lost their livelihoods and moved their families to the mainland. In the past ten years, Tilting has lost one third of its population, and today there are about 350 residents. Those residents who remain in Tilting are determined to make the best of it. Fishers who were able to diversify and fish for other species like crab and turbot have been able to carry on in hard times. Although in recent years the preservation of its built heritage has become a priority, Tilting remains a dynamic, living, working community, not a static heritage village.

In Tilting's harbor the presence of the sea predominates in summer, but in winter it is the ice. The harbor is frozen and covered with snow, as are the ponds and marshes in the surrounding area. In winter harvesting wood is the main outdoor activity and a full-time, daily job for men. It begins in mid-November or early December when the marshes and ponds freeze. Dorothy Burke told me that in the past, men would go into the woods in groups to cut paths and harvest wood. They would leave after dawn, and come back in early afternoon. This schedule continued until late March or early April.

The slide paths for wood harvesting reach as far as the south coast of the island, and each pond, pinch, marsh, ridge, neck, pass, droke, height, and barren has a name. In the days of slide hauling with horses, in order to visually assist in following the paths in poor weather,

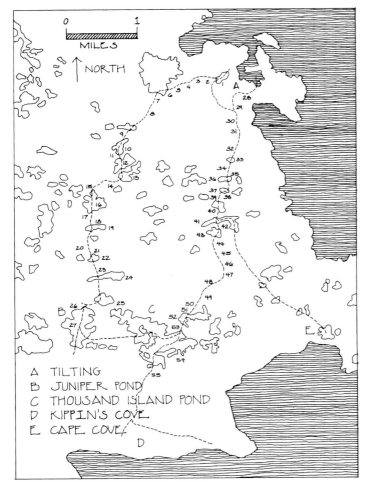

A TILTING
B JUNIPER POND
C THOUSAND ISLAND POND
D KIPPIN'S COVE
E CAPE COVE

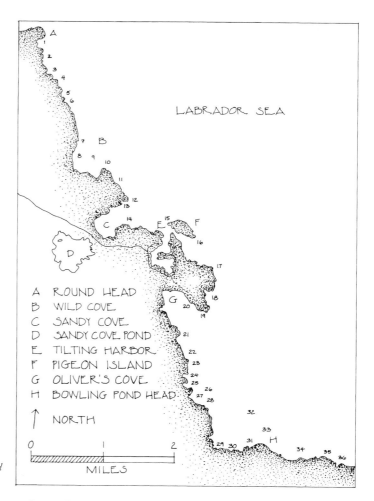

LABRADOR SEA

A ROUND HEAD
B WILD COVE
C SANDY COVE
D SANDY COVE POND
E TILTING HARBOR
F PIGEON ISLAND
G OLIVER'S COVE
H BOWLING POND HEAD

↑ NORTH

0   1   2
|////////////////////|
MILES

Traditional cod trap berths located close to the shore near Tilting

Index to cod trap berths:

1. Round Head Cove
2. Long Point
3. Northern Yellow Gulch
4. Southern Yellow Gulch
5. Green Gulch
6. Ambrose McGrath's Point
7. Bob's Gulch
8. Pat Keefe's Gulch
9. Wild Cove Point
10. Wild Cove
11. Wild Cove Rock
12. Sandy Cove Head
13. Sweeney's Rocks
14. Black Rock
15. Western Point
16. Eastern Point Tickle
17. Careless Point

18. Pummely Cove
19. Rock of the Head
20. Mike Keefe's Point
21. Long Point
22. Tuck Sunker
23. Mansfield Point
24. Broaders' Gulch
25. Shanahan's Point
26. The Blowing Hole
27. Katin's Head
28. Island Rock of Katin's Head
29. Higgins' Gulch
30. Cronin's Gulch
31. Humperelle Gulch
32. The Bar
33. Bowling Pond Head
34. The High Head
35. The Breaking Rocks
36. The Fishing Gulch

DAN GREENE ON BOUGHING PATHS: We were in there twenty below when you wouldn't see with vapor. Wasn't snow, it was vapor. A storm of wind—blowing forty, fifty mile of wind—there was never anything like it—fellows crossed the pond and everything. But we had it boughed right from over here to of Keefe's to the bottom of Kippin's Cove, you couldn't get astray. You left the top on the bough—you'd see that black top. It would break out of it—one bough to the other, fir and spruce. After the holes were cut, water was thrown on the hole to freeze the bough in overnight.

paths were "boughed" where they crossed ponds.[19] Boughs were small "longers" or narrow tree trunks about eight or ten feet long, with limbs removed except for the top ones, which were planted in holes in the ice at regular intervals along the paths. Boughing and maintaining the paths was a cooperative effort. Everyone had to participate to make it work.

Slide hauling with horses can be tricky and dangerous. I was not aware of just how difficult it is to keep a fully loaded slide on the path until I made a wood harvesting trip with Andrew and Neil McGrath to the south coast of Fogo Island. This was in the late 1980s, when the McGrath family still had Brandy, their Newfoundland pony. From this trip I learned about the hazards of crossing the ponds, of blizzards known as whiteouts, of the slippery conditions on hills, and of the difficulty of controlling the horse's enthusiasm when getting close to home. After a full day out in the cold, Gladys McGrath, Andrew and Neil's mother, made us delicious toutons (pan-cooked bread dough) and tea on the wood stove in her cozy back kitchen.

Before horses were used for slide hauling in Tilting, many families used dogs. Albert and Theresa Foley told me they had two dogs for hauling their bunker slide, and each required nine doughboys (dumplings made with flour) a day. Dogs were used for hauling small loads of firewood, fence pickets, and water. Dan Greene told me that crannick wood, wood that was small, short, crooked, and boxy, was often collected by using man-powered hand slides before the start of the regular slide hauling season. He used to do this late in the fall around Donovan's Ridge, Clance's Neck, and Mickel's Pond.

Snowshoes were essential for hauling wood in the winter, and these were locally made with bentwood frames and leather and twine

Neil McGrath and Brandy crossing a pond on the way back to Tilting

DAN GREENE ON SLIDE HAULING: Some of the horses would become crazy down Palmer's, see? They'd break into a gallop and some fellows would have to let go of the reins and get clear of the wood and let it go on—they didn't have time. At the bottom of Palmers everything would be beat up—the load of wood upset and beat to pieces. I used to back down the hill—the fellow that would back him, he would back that load of wood down Palmer's. You'd just know there was a slide moving—and you way out clear with the reins hauled back and your two heels stuck in and he backing it—some of the horses you couldn't get them to back.

Ted Burke with the pair of locally made snowshoes that saved
Alonzo Saunder's life in a severe snow storm on Fogo Island

webbing. Ted Burke showed me a pair of locally made snowshoes that
saved Alonzo Saunder's life. He was walking from Cape Cove to
Seldom when he was caught in a severe snowstorm, and he would never
have made it without the snowshoes. Not everyone had snowshoes,
so potlids made from boards were often used instead. They were used
off the slide path for cutting and "spelling" wood (carrying a heavy
stick of wood on your back).

Schooners and bully boats were used to bring in wood from off
the island. In the early settlement of Tilting, when houses had open
fireplaces, John Carroll traveled by schooner deep in Notre Dame Bay
to "cruise wood." If there was a northeast wind on the return journey,
you could not sail home, turning a short trip of a few days into weeks.
Later, the use of engines made trips off the island more predictable.
Usually there were four or five men on each schooner trip, and each
got a share of the wood.

Neat woodpiles are a matter of pride, contributing to the general
impression of well-maintained premises. Dan Greene is one of the

Two of Dan Greene's woodpiles behind his house. To the right is his wood store and stable.

most skilful residents in the harbor at stacking wood, and he told me about the advantages and disadvantages of different types of woodpiles. Before the wood is junked (cut into stove-length pieces) and split, you stack long pieces of wood vertically by making a wigwam pile. This will allow the wood to dry well and allow you to find it in the snow. First, you place a center post in the ground and brace this with diagonal supports. Then you carefully balance wood all around this post, with the butt end of the wood in contact with the ground. This is one of the most common types of traditional woodpiles in Tilting. Variations include the strongback, a heavy horizontal log braced like a trestle that supports the wood in a high tentlike shape, and also stacking wood against cliffs and the gable ends of outbuildings. Once the wood is junked, it is stacked in perfectly square or round piles, satisfying to behold and easy to monitor. If you need to quickly dry your wood, you make a long narrow pile like a wall to ensure good cross ventilation.

Wood was not the only fuel harvested for heating houses in Tilting. Fergus Dwyer used to cut peat in the fall of the year, when

TED BURKE ON GUNNING: In my day, and in my great-grandfather's day, you could take the gun, you could go down, you could kill your meal of birds, anytime at all—there was nothing to drive them. I seen hundreds and hundreds of ducks in the one flock—and it was just the same as if I had a flock of hens out there roamin' around. But you won't see it today. We were in Cape—I gunned a lifetime, certainly I did—seals, ducks, and everything. I had everything down there then—I had the stable down there, the store—house down there—and we had a punt down there. And we'd go down—we'd kill sixty, and seventy, and eighty—all we wanted. We'd put 'em on our horse—come on up—no troubles—and—the last three or four year I was at it—they got the skidoos. Two fellows from Joe Batt's Arm was the first two to have skidoos—and they come down here—and me, and Just Burke, and Alan, and Watt, and Mick—was out after this shot of ducks—Sunday evening it was—and—we didn't care what day it was—and still, boy—you'd hear anyone talkin' up here. Now, by and by I said, "I hears the head queer noise." We didn't know anything about skidoos—there's not a plane—and as we're talkin' the ducks went to wing and we never got a shot at 'em. And by and by these fellows were out on top of us on skidoos—and I said to the boys, I said, "now my son, you can hang up your socks—Cape is finished—you'll never get another duck—only chance if you're there and got the chance to kill one, or got the chance to kill two—you got to fire—and if you don't, you'll come home without a bird." And 'twas true as the life—could be a shot of ducks out at the Wester' Point, and I go out here again' the door and start a skidoo, that's all I got to do—they're gone.

firewood was scarce, at Pummely Cove Pond. Alice Greene told me a man from Bonavista came to Tilting in 1940 to show people how to make peat on Tate's Marsh, but this never became common practice in the community.[20]

When not occupied with slide hauling, men would also go gunning (for birds), hunting (for big game), and snaring (for rabbits). From late October to the end of April was the gunning season for saltwater ducks, and from November to the last of March was the season for partridge. As Ted Burke described it, in Cape Cove, "you could kill all the ducks you like. We killed sixty one night at the stage in December." Cape Cove residents used to host Tilting residents at "duck suppers," social evenings of food, music, and dancing. Caribou hunting on Fogo Island started in 1963, and some men who worked in the lumber woods off Fogo Island hunted for moose. Rabbit snaring season was from November to March. Ted Burke said you should never set a rabbit slip until the end of November, and slips were taken up March 1 to prevent destruction of the rabbit population.

In the nineteenth century, people from Tilting went to the ice in schooners to get seals. Years later men from Tilting would go out in punts to net seals in the spring of the year. Frank Mahoney recalled netting seals in April off Careless Point, The Easter Tickle, Oliver's Cove, and Sandy Cove Bight using ten- and twelve-inch cotton mesh. Others traveled to St. John's to go to the ice with a sealing captain. Dan Greene's father went sealing to the ice with the famous Captain Abraham Kean for twenty-five springs.

Seals were only a sideline in Tilting. They usually did not land in Tilting and were typically thirty miles offshore in the location known as The Cut. Only twice in Pearce Dwyer's memory were seals hauled from the ice around Tilting in any quantity. In 1944, the ice was covered with seals as a northeasterly wind drove them inshore, and each family got between fifteen to twenty seals. When outboard motors became available, people went out to get seals. The closure of Newfoundland's seal fishery a few years ago did not affect Tilting's

TED BURKE ON HARD TIMES: At that time, they used to give out a little bit of relief, now—damn small lot. I seen families in Cape Cove what they used to get—bit of brown flour, bit of rolled oats, drop of molasses, bit of brown sugar, bit of hard bread. Well, my son—I hope it will never happen again. And another thing, we knew nothing. The merchants—we knew nothing—we didn't know how much the merchant was reaping off of us—we had nothing to show. They could give us just what they liked—you could carry up a quintal of number one fish, and they could give you just what they liked. But today, by the middle of March you'll have your fishing form coming. The price of every pound of fish is on it.

Joe Eaton's house in Cape Cove

way of life, but it did affect those who would go to St. John's every spring to go to the ice.

Berry picking was an important seasonal activity in Tilting. The first crop of bakeapples, found on the marshes around Tilting, were harvested around August 10. On the barrens blueberries were picked from mid-August until the first frost, and partridgeberries from late August until the end of September. Raspberries were ripe by mid-August, and could be found in places like Palmer's and the Morris Lyon's Cove Hills.

Hauling fresh water was a year-round activity in Tilting. Pearce Dwyer described the daily routine when he was growing up near The Rock. Each day he made three trips by foot from his house, either to Oliver's Cove, to The Washing Ponds, or to Sweeney's Gulch. He used three gallon buckets balanced on a water hoop. People also went to Sandy Cove Pond to get water; in winter they would travel by horse and slide, and in summer by boat. When I was doing my fieldwork in Tilting, I had to drive out on the ice of Sandy Cove Pond to get my water. Most households collected rainwater from roofs for use in washing. Pearce Dwyer's house used to have a wooden chute on the eave of the back kitchen roof for this purpose. By the end of 2001, most houses in Tilting were connected to the public water supply.

Tilting's traditional way of life was in balance with its available natural resources. Though the architecture of Tilting separated itself from nature, the materials and the construction processes buildings used had little impact on the environment in terms of pollution, energy requirements, and use of materials. The two main subsistence activities of the residents, the inshore fishery and agriculture, demonstrate this balance.

The traditional inshore fishery practices of Tilting's residents did not have much of an impact on the decline of the cod stocks compared to the practices of the large offshore fishing draggers. By the time Canada declared a two-hundred-mile limit and a moratorium on fishing for cod, it was too late. The recovery of the cod stocks has been disappointing, and it is not known if they will ever recover.

Disintegrating fishing stage foundations and bedding on Greene's Point: Gerard Greene's stage (left) and Dan Greene's stage (right)

Tilting's sub-Arctic climate is not the most hospitable for crops, and its soil conditions were very poor. But techniques were developed over several generations to build up the soil and to store root crops in structures that were compatible with the cold climate. The practice of open field grazing for cows, sheep, and horses worked very well, permitting animals to forage for seasonal indigenous vegetation with little or no cost for animal feed. In Tilting even home heating was in balance with nature. Energy was conserved by heating only the part of the house closest to the wood stove. If you were cold, you added another layer of clothing.

It took courage and phenomenal endurance to survive in this inhospitable landscape and climate. Fogo Islanders have always been renowned for their energy, agility, and stamina, for their ability to accomplish extraordinary feats of work in a short time. This related to the very short season on Fogo Island for fishing, agriculture, and construction. Much had to be accomplished in a short period of time before the start of winter.

In contrast to the ruggedness of its landscape and the strength of its people, Tilting's architecture can be described as fragile, "concerned with real sensory interaction instead of idealized and conceptual manifestations."[21] Although formal, symmetrical, and tripartite forms appear in its house facades, furniture, and hooked mats, Tilting's architecture is malleable and expansive, opening up instead of closing down. This can be seen in house and furniture additions and transformations, and also in the correspondences between details and materials for houses, outbuildings, fences, and tools. It is also evident in the way many residents of Tilting do their own construction work and maintain their own houses, outbuildings, fishing premises, and gardens.

In Tilting's architecture fragility is especially evident in the ecological aspect of building. It is commonly understood that fences and fishing stages and flakes, built mainly with wood, would have to be rebuilt two or three times in one's lifetime. Their basic construction was forgiving and used local materials that were easy to work with and fairly elastic. If a storm wrecked a fishing stage, materials could often be retrieved and recycled for use in the construction of a new stage. Windstorms and ice pressures could damage and deform structures, but they could often be repaired instead of completely rebuilt. The wood and stone cribbing system used for stage wharves was easy to build and worked much more efficiently than heavily reinforced concrete wharves for resisting deformations from ice pressures. Houses and outbuildings were often moved to other sites to be reused by someone else if they were no longer needed. Even parts of houses—windows, doors, and floor beams—could be moved and recycled. When Ed McGrath's house was demolished a few years ago, the back kitchen was moved to Len McGrath's premises, where he presently uses it as a store.

Houses and stages that were no longer used or maintained would sometimes practically melt into the landscape over time. The ecological aspect of this disintegration is obvious. Since the building's light wood foundation did not cut into or mark the landscape in any way, no evidence of construction would remain after the buildings crumbled, leaving the

Ed McGrath's back kitchen. On the left, it is still intact during the demolition of his house. On the right, it has been launched to Len McGrath's premises for use as a storage outbuilding.

landscape virtually unchanged. It is this aspect of Tilting's construction that is remarkably fragile: houses, outbuildings, stages, and flakes constructed with wood foundations that carefully supported and balanced the superstructure over rugged, irregular terrain, and left no traces.

Fragility also characterizes Tilting's cultural landscape. The settlement developed from incremental growth based on the experiential knowledge and use of the terrain, combined with land-use patterns influenced by family structure, social conventions, and work, rather than a purposeful, overall plan.

Tilting's architecture and cultural landscape resulted from subsistence farming, a cooperative way of life, and the use of environmentally low-impact technology. Renovations, additions, and repairs to houses were easy to do, and people were able to creatively improvise and make many of the things they needed. Houses were modest in size, and public life was more important than the private hoarding of possessions in a large house. House form was egalitarian, and everyone knew what everyone else had by way of possessions. As in the case of mat making, what was admired was not what you purchased but rather what you accomplished with your own hands. Today, this lifestyle has largely disappeared in most places in North America.

They don't bother to knock—because everybody around here knows one another and they knows what's in there and they knows what kind of a person they're going to meet and—there's no need of them knocking—I think that's the reason. Everyone is welcome here—all the people that I know in Tilting that I'm acquainted with that I'm used to—I'd just as soon go in their kitchen as go across the road—that's the way I feel about it and I know they'd feel the same thing about me. Someone coming in, it's only Jim—no odds about him—that's the way most people look at it. Nobody don't want to take off their boots—We had several people comin' in stopped out in the porch tryin' to get off their boots—come on in, boy!

You know Mark Foley? He was away into St. John's and I met him one day—I said, "Mark, you were gone." He said, "Yes boy, I was into St. John's and I had a spell takin' off me boots." Why, that's bullshit! They're imitating that crowd in St. John's and that's the reason—we're going to be just like the crowd that's in St. John's and you got to do the same thing in their houses as they does in St. John's—full of bull. I had a pair of boots one time I couldn't get off—what'll I do then? You knows the kind of boots they are—they calls them "flits" and they calls them "unemployment boots"—them rubbers with a couple of laces up at the top. I bought a pair one time and I put them on—didn't have much trouble to get them on—but in the evening when I went to get them off I couldn't get them off. I lay down on the floor and I hauled on them and everything and I couldn't get them off—after a while I got them off, and I never put them on no more. Another fellow down there, Billy Broaders, he's dead now, he put a pair on one time he had to cut his off! Well, if you're going to their house with them boots on you have to turn around and come back—you couldn't get in, could you?

CHAPTER 2

HOUSE FORM AND VISITING

----

*W*HEN I FIRST ARRIVED IN TILTING, my goal was to measure and record each house in the community, old and new.[1] I could have saved a lot of time by selecting only a few houses, but in almost every house I learned something new from a conversation, a piece of furniture, or an old photograph. Also, by visiting every house I had the opportunity to meet everyone in the community. At first, I was known around the harbor as the "strange man." Fortunately, after a few months, when people got used to me, "strange man" was replaced by "Robert."

Most of the older houses still standing in Tilting were built in the late nineteenth and early twentieth centuries. They were typically two-story houses with either gable or low-pitched roofs, and only their exterior walls were load bearing. Their foundations were wooden posts or shores, and these required occasional maintenance after settlement or decay. The interior walls were made of vertically placed, single thickness, tongue-and-groove board, which saved space and could be easily relocated. The framing of these houses was similar to balloon-frame construction, with wall studs spanning from the foundation sill plates to the roof eaves and with ledgers to support the ends of the second floor joists. In houses with gable roofs, like the Reardon house in Sandy Cove, the second-floor ceiling joists also acted as collar ties for the rafters. Wood shingles with a narrow, regular coursing were used on gable-roof houses.

The Reardon house was part of a small enclave of houses and outbuildings that was completely fenced in to keep grazing animals out. It was the last house in Sandy Cove, and Gerald Reardon was using it as a stable when I made my drawings of it. All the partitions on the ground floor had been removed, and the loft was being used to store hay. It was in very poor condition and in danger of collapsing. In 2001 the Tilting Cultural and Recreation Society completely restored this house, and it now stands in testament to Tilting's older houses.

The front gate of the Kinsella premises. Albert Cluett told me that in his opinion a house does not feel complete without a proper fence around it.

Jack Reardon's house in Sandy Cove when Gerald Reardon was using it as a stable

The exterior employs four-inch exposure clapboards, wide wood window and door trim, and wood roof shingles. The second-floor windows can be raised only a few inches for ventilation. A mantelpiece, the heavy beam in the first-floor ceiling, supports a masonry chimney. Wherever possible, heavy timbers were left "in the round" to provide extra strength and reduce the time required to prepare timber for construction. The Reardon house is one of the few houses in Tilting constructed with a "purlined" roof. Purlins are small support members that span directly above and perpendicular to the rafters, permitting the roof sheathing boards to follow the slope of the roof.

The Reardon house shows the typical interior finish of Tilting's houses. The interior faces of the exterior walls are carefully sheathed

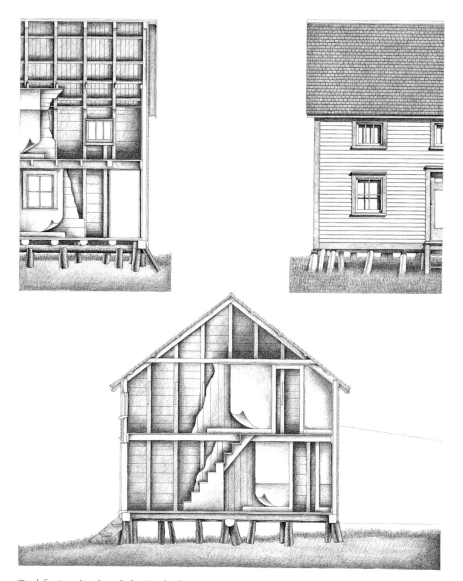

Top left: A section through the Reardon house in Sandy Cove, showing the purlined roof construction (locally described as rafters with "stringers")

Top right: The front of the Reardon house in Sandy Cove. The posts or shores under the house were the main foundation supports, permitting the house to be moved or "launched" with ease.

Bottom: A cross section through the Reardon house in Sandy Cove. Whenever possible, heavy timbers were left "in the round" to provide extra strength and to reduce the time required to prepare materials for construction.

TED BURKE ON VISITING: I'll tell you the answer to it all: 'tis all carpet now, and they don't want the sheep to go handy—afraid they'd be treading in a bit of sheep shit—to bring it in on their carpet. But at that time, everyone was alike—there was an old canvas mat or a rag mat and you could wipe your boots and come on in. But now today, you got to take off your boots, out on the gallery. Years ago, I minds to count thirty-two people here one night—well, some of them brought in the snow—that was in the winter—and we never sung out, "Brush your boots" or nothing—'twas only a clean drop of water. They could come on in—no such thing as taking off your boots.

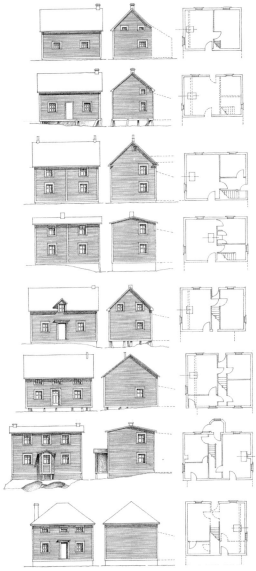

A housing typology for the older houses found in Tilting. Shown from top to bottom are the Duff house, Allan Keefe's store (formerly a house), Dorothy Burke's house, Ned Cluett's house, Frank Mahoney's house, the Reardon house in Sandy Cove, the Kinsella house, and Mark and Catherine Foley's house.

FRANK MAHONEY ON HOUSE TYPES: You can look at all the houses around now, because they're nearly the same fashion—clear of the flat roof ones, and they're a kind of a new come up.

with tongue-and-groove boards, and the joints of these boards (and also the partition boards) are covered with narrow strips of linen. Layers of newspaper are applied next, using a paste made from flour and water, and this newspaper becomes the surface for wallpaper. On the second floor, these papered low walls combine with exposed, painted joists to provide an intimate and congenial character for the rooms. Plain but substantial baseboards and window and door trim were used throughout these houses, and kitchens often had a wooden wainscot or chair rail. Floors were bare, painted, or covered with layers of heavy, painted cotton canvas like sailcloth or linoleum. The second floor had a "coped" or "cooped" ceiling, which limited headroom but allowed for construction economy and energy conservation. The lower ceiling heights of the bedrooms were well proportioned for their small area, which could usually only accommodate a bed and a small dresser.

Tilting's older houses fall into two types: a hall (kitchen)-and-parlor (living room or "the room") plan with the main entrance on the gable-end side, and a slightly larger center-hall plan with the main entrance roughly in the middle of the front facade and a steep central stair.[2] The kitchen, usually accessed through the back porch, was the center of daily life and visiting. Kitchens were usually wider and larger in area than parlors. On the front of the house, windows and doors were placed to try to balance the awkwardness of the front room's different widths. Front facades are thus made symmetrical, with a tripartite placement of windows, doors, and trim boards. Hall and parlor–plan houses typically had three bedrooms on the second floor. Center hall–plan houses had an extra room on the first floor that was used as a pantry, and there were usually four small bedrooms on the second floor. Some center hall–plan houses had a small stairway, either open or enclosed, leading to an attic.

In the old house, low ceilings help to keep the house warm by reducing the heated volume of the house, and low ceilings also reduce

The front door of Harold Dwyer's house, formerly Allan and Mary Keefe's front door. This door has false wood graining.

Opposite and above: A typology of additions to old houses in Tilting. Shown from left to right are the gable-roof porch of the McKenna house (demolished), Justin Foley's back kitchen, a partial two-story addition to Mike and Marie Greene's house, a full two-story addition to Gilbert Dwyer's house, a side addition to Austin and Kate Foley's house, a transforming side addition to Allan and Millicent Dwyer's house, and a transforming front addition to Joe Burke's house.

the quantity of house construction materials. Although it is commonly assumed that Tilting's early residents were short, Fergus Broders disputes this. When Fergus and I measured Cyril and Julia Dwyer's house, he mentioned the Dwyers were not short. The house was built between 1880 and 1890 by William Dwyer. All the doors downstairs were only five and a half feet high, while the ceilings on both floors were six and a quarter feet high.

The old house was not considered complete without the construction of additions. All the older houses in Tilting had additions of one kind or another, some with many distinct parts that were built incrementally over time to accommodate changing family requirements. These included storage areas, washhouses, back porches, bedrooms, and back kitchens. Many had their roofs modified from steep-pitched gable roofs to low-pitched roofs, and others had their second floors removed entirely. Except for houses that originally had an "inside" porch (a porch located within the main volume of the house), an addition to the back of the house was indispensable. The minimum addition was a back porch, and this would be constructed at the same time as the house.

In the early part of the twentieth century, back kitchens started to replace back porches. Early back kitchen additions were small and were used mainly for eating meals in summer and storage in winter. They were entered from outside through a small porch or vestibule. In this arrangement, the back kitchen was thought of as an "outside" kitchen, and the old kitchen became known as the "inside" kitchen. They are an extension of the informality of the outdoor area behind the house where daily tasks like cutting firewood and hanging up laundry occur. In the large back kitchen, the occupants of the house live behind the house in their idea of casual comfort: a place where

Mike McGrath with his nieces on the bridge leading to the back door of his house (from left to right, Chantel Glover, Jill McGrath, and Amy McGrath). Mike, a bachelor, fished with his brothers in a family fishing crew.

visitors can come in without formality. As back kitchens got larger, they were often occupied year round.

According to Jim Greene, the reason for the large back kitchen was "to try to make everything grand." The main part of the house was reserved for visits by special guests like strangers or the clergy, and was protected by the back kitchen from everyday use. The "inside" kitchen, now superfluous, gradually became a "living room."[3] This left the question of what to do with "the room." "The room" was even further removed from the everyday realm of the kitchen than it was before, and it eventually became vulnerable to changes of use and renovations. But when the large back kitchen was first introduced, "the room" still maintained its status as a more formal room suitable for display, special visits, and wakes, despite competition for visitors from the inside kitchen.

Clarence Foley told me one visitor's impression of the old houses in Tilting: "They builds a house—and then they builds a place in back of it to live in." This terse but astute observation calls attention to the importance of additions to houses in the community. Until recent years additions would never upset the integrity of the front facade of a Tilting house or transform the house core. Some houses had additions

TED BURKE ON VISITING IN CAPE COVE: You would not have much of a ball, but you'd have a card game, and you'd have something cooked. You'd have no dances with the crowd that's there cause there wouldn't have been enough, you see. Perhaps three or four fellows would come to the house, like Sam or Art—and have a drink of beer—and by and by when you get to feeling O.K. someone would say, "Sam, what about singing us a song?" They were wonderful singers, you see. And when he'd be finished, then the other fellow would sing. Bye and bye 'twould be time to get a lunch—fellows down there could say recitations. Bernard Cluett used to be a wonderful sport—'twas three or four down there could play the accordion and the violin—'twas never a man said a cross word to each other.

to the side, but most were to the back. There was a period of transforming additions to the front of the house just before residents started to build new ranch and split-level houses, sometimes making the old houses look like these new types. This indicates that even in recent times Tilting residents preferred reusing an old house to demolition.

When no longer needed, old houses could be reused as outbuildings. Gilbert Dwyer's twine loft was originally a house built by John Ellsworth around 1872. Before it became a twine loft, it was a store[4] and then a cod liver oil factory. It was also used for pit-sawing lumber and for building boats; Phonse and Joe Dwyer built twenty-five boats in it. This building was moved three times, and its roof was cut down from a gable roof to a flat roof.

Although Tilting's old houses may seem small to us, the owners did not think of them that way. They were thought to be fairly spacious compared to the very small nineteenth-century houses in Tilting, none of which remain today. Only one of these houses, the Davis house, was still standing when I arrived in Tilting. For many years it served as a storage area behind Hurley's old false-fronted retail store. You could barely stand up in the second-floor loft of the house. Before the house and store were demolished, I saved a piece of the second-floor stair wooden guardrail: it was only eighteen inches high.

There were other small houses like the Davis house with saltbox-shaped roofs. Mildred Hurley and Donald Foley told me about one of these, the John Power house. Located along the road to Oliver's Cove, it was very small and had two windows at the front on the first

Oh, yes—I always does it. That's the way we always done
it. Say, "I'll see you later" or "good luck" or—I think it's
my place to follow him to the door and bid him good day—
I likes to be fair with everyone.

floor, a window in each gable end for the second-floor bedrooms, and
a central stair. Dan Greene described the Duff house, which had a ship's
ladder off the kitchen instead of a stair to the second floor, and was
located near the Power house. The wood for this house was cut in Sand
Cove Forest near Oliver's Cove. Fergus Burke said the Duff house had
open shelves on the wall, possibly like a kitchen dresser with luster jugs,
different color mugs, and antique plates on display. In the kitchen there
was a Waterloo stove. Both the Duff house and the Power house were
"full studded," that is, constructed with load-bearing exterior walls
of vertical studs placed tightly together.

Although there are many similarities of form and layout between
Tilting's nineteenth-century houses and rural houses in Ireland, it is
not possible to trace a direct transfer of house types from the old country
to Tilting in the way John Mannion documented earlier authentic
transfers from Ireland to the Avalon Peninsula.[5] There were undoubtedly
English and Irish influences on house form in Tilting, but also influences
from the Maritimes and New England. For example, Gerald Dwyer,
Harold Dwyer's grandfather, worked in the mines in Nova Scotia in the
late 1800s. He saw a curved, bell-cast shaped roof that he liked, and
used this design for his own house in Tilting.[6]

Tilting's oldest existing houses are similar in scale to small houses
in Devon, England, and the Tidewater area of Chesapeake Bay, Virginia.
Some of the more recent twentieth-century variations of these houses
are reminiscent of small houses in New England.[7] When Lambert
Greene came home from working in Boston, the houses he saw there
influenced the design of his house in Tilting. Jim Greene worked in
Boston also, and his house is similar to Lambert's.

John Mannion believes the reason small houses were constructed
in Tilting was cultural, not a matter of wealth. People were more

Gilbert Dwyer outside the outbuilding he once used as a cod liver oil factory

Left: The Davis house attached to the back of Hurley's old retail store
Right: Harold Dwyer's house, the house my family purchased in 1987. Gerald Reardon was responsible for most of the restoration work on the exterior, and Pearce Dwyer and his family did much of the work on the interior.

interested in life outside the house, in boats and in fishing, and had different ideas of family and privacy from those we are accustomed to today. Families were large, and it was common for several children to share a bed. Although parents had their own bedrooms, acoustical privacy was impossible with single-board partition walls. Just walking across the second floor of an old house makes the floor bounce, and this can be felt by everyone upstairs. If extra people like sharemen had to be accommodated during the fishing season, they slept in "shanty lofts," the lofts of twine stores, and sometimes even in the attics of houses.

The basic form of Tilting's two main older house types was egalitarian,[8] indicating that everyone had the same status except for the parish priest and "the merchant."[9] The house with the highest status was typically the parish house, but in Tilting the merchant's house— occupied by the Bryan family, schooner builders and later local agents for Earle's—was always considered to be of higher status. Today the parish priest lives in a modest new two-story house, and a merchant's agent no longer resides in the community.

Ben and Annie Foley's house in Tilting is the first instance I have seen in Newfoundland of the use of a false front door. It became a source of amusement when strangers would knock on it. A non-load-bearing, single-board partition between the kitchen and parlor intersected the front door. Originally, the door had three panels, carved brackets above, and according to its current owners, "It had a knob and everything." There was never any hint of the door on the inside of the house. Len Carroll started construction on this house in 1927, but it was never finished. Ben and Annie purchased the house in March 1942. The plan of the house followed the hall-and-parlor design, but the designer of the exterior of the house aspired to the center-hall design.

When I asked Jim Greene about false front doors, he seemed to think there were other houses that had them in Tilting as well.[10] He told me false front doors were for "making out that the house was so big: only just a bluff. Making out that everything was there just like in the bigger houses." Some residents of old houses dispensed with their front doors since they mainly used the back door. Gilbert Dwyer told

ANNIE FOLEY ON CHRISTMAS ENTERTAINMENT: I see mom, after Christmas night, after midnight mass, and she with the big roast in the oven—Uncle Joe would bring in three or four fellows with him. They'd be there and have a few drinks, songs, and reciting and all that—and dad would say, "Well boys, you're hungry now." Bridge, set the table and get them something to eat. And they'd set the table, just the same as for breakfast or for supper, whatever it would be, cut off the bread, get out the big roast— roast was in a great big iron pot, and cut off the fresh beef—and give a piece of fresh beef each, and sit down and eat their fill. I don't think you'd get no one to do that today, you know? Now, that's the way they used to do it. And that would be over then, clear off the dishes, and someone amongst the crowd may have a mouth organ, or an accordion, and they'd say, "Anyone know how to dance the lancer?" That was a dance. So it ended up they'd have to take all those mats off the floor and get out and have a dance. The lancer, or a reel, or a square dance—a lot of people could dance then—pull back all the chairs and take out the table and push it in the room or in the hall. Father and mother would be interested—she'd get out in it. But dad usen't to get out in it. He'd be so interested in that! He'd sit up in the corner and he'd laugh his belly full. There was wonderful people then. I suppose there was nothing else to entertain them then, boy. No televisions or nothing then.

You'd lay the pan down, tie on the dancin' master, and you'd have nails in his feet—little tacks in his heels, and when he'd tip it out—boy! And the better you could play and sing the tune, keep time—*I can do it very good meself.*

me about the removal of his front door: "The old fellow who built the house thought it would look better with a front door in it, but I didn't—there was no use to it, you see."

There are a broader range of house types found in Tilting today, old and new. The main change to the new house is its larger area and height. The advent of central heating made the construction of bigger one-story bungalows and split levels possible. Heat from the kitchen wood stove used in the old house made this unfeasible.

In Tilting there is little evidence of a gradual transition from old to new house types.[11] Until well into the 1960s, traditional two-story houses were still constructed in Tilting, and only two single-level bungalows were built before 1970. Gerald Dwyer's house, a large two-story center-hall house with a gable roof and white clapboards, was constructed in 1950. This house originally had narrow clapboards, locally made windows and doors, masonry chimneys, and wood roof shingles. Dan and Marie Foley's house, built by Dan when he was twenty-one in 1963, was the last of the traditional two-story house types to be constructed in Tilting. It is remarkable how long this type of house construction persisted in Tilting, considering that new bungalow-type houses had been constructed elsewhere in Newfoundland beginning in the late 1920s. The Foley house had no insulation, and it was similar to the house Dan grew up in, presently occupied by his brother Justin. In 1976, Dan covered the front door on the inside but he left it intact on the outside to retain the original appearance of the house.

Between 1961 and 1972, just before the start of Tilting's new house construction period, the fishery in Tilting was poor and the family crews who were trap fishing were hit hard. Each neighborhood lost residents who moved elsewhere to look for work. Unemployment benefits were inadequate, there were few fishers in the harbor, and no employment opportunities for young people. Few houses were built then because there was a sufficient stock of old houses. When the fishery

Ben and Annie Foley's house with a false front door. People not familiar with the house would knock on this door, which had "a knob and everything."

BEN AND ANNIE FOLEY ON CHRISTMAS: [Ben] 'Twas twelve days celebrated then, years ago. You could go where you like, Christmas. The understood thing was to keep up the twelve days. And it gradually died out and died out and if you were here—if you comes back here another three or four years, you won't know it's Christmas here. No mummers comin' in no more—not many lets them in, so its no good goin' out now. [Annie] Your neighbors would come down Christmas eve, and you'd have a drink and, they'd be keep alright till twelve o'clock after midnight mass—that'd be the word now, don't drink too much till after the midnight mass. [Ben] There would be an excitement to it then, boy—every night there was a party, sure—you can go down to that club, sure, and stay as long as you like, there's no excitement or nothing. [Annie] What would you have for Christmas that you don't have every other day now? This is another thing. You'd have sweet bread at Christmas, and you wouldn't have no more until next Christmas. And everything was a treat. There's sweet bread every day now.

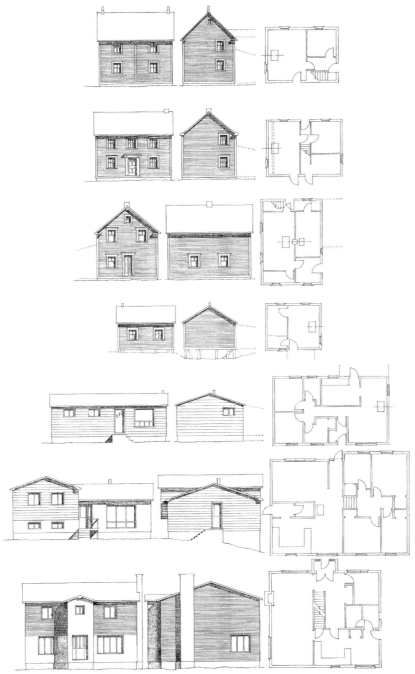

A housing typology of old and new houses in Tilting. Shown from top to bottom are a hall-and-parlor house, a center hall–plan house, a house with the gable end facing the road, a transitional-house type constructed for senior citizens that retains aspects of the old hall-and-parlor plan, Fergus Burke's bungalow, Cyril and Paula McGrath's split-level, and Gerard and Maxine Greene's two-story house.

MARTIN GREENE ON FALSE FRONT DOORS:

There was a door in the middle on the front. But they never used it. It was just imitation. Understand? They never used that door but the door was there. You couldn't open it—it was just a door. You going down the road and you look—and he had a front door but he wasn't using that front door. 'Twas just an imitation of it.

improved, people who had been forced to leave the community to find work started to return.[12] They brought with them popular house influences from elsewhere in Newfoundland and Canada, and house building resumed in the community.

Isolation may explain the absence of new types of house construction in the 1950s, and government pressure to resettle Fogo Islanders and a poor fishery may account for the lack of much new house construction during the 1960s. The first bungalow was constructed in 1961, the first split-level house in 1972, and the first new two-story house in 1984. Of the forty-four owners of larger new houses I was able to interview, only three had mortgages and thirty-seven had done substantial construction work on their houses. Basil Lane built the first bungalow in the harbor, and he was influenced by houses he saw while traveling. His house always had only one exterior door at the front, and it used to have a hallway in the center nearly the length of the house. Three bedrooms are located along the back of the house, and there is a kitchen, dining room, and living room along the front. Although the builders of new houses in Tilting had access to mail order plans and government housing agency plans, most either drew their own plans, modified existing plans, or copied the layout of a neighbor's house.

New houses are not launched when they are sold. They are usually committed to their sites by concrete foundations and landscaping, and their size and construction make them difficult to move. They are oriented to face the road, with a large front lawn placed between the road and the house if possible. Views of the harbor from the principal rooms are a secondary consideration if thought of at all.

Some builders of new houses elected to remain in the community near their families, but others preferred some separation from the

DAN GREENE ON WAKES: The trouble with a wake if a person died in a new bungalow is you wouldn't get the corpse out. You wouldn't get the coffin in or out the way those houses are built. You can't turn: there's no room. In some houses, the coffin had to be taken out through the window—feet first—that's the way you're walking, just the same as if you're stood up walking. A lot of them fellows tangled up their doors, see? They built houses and they remarked that when you died they won't get you out of it. Wakes have gone out, see? That's the way it was done all our life and my father's time—everybody was waken at home and carried to the church. You can't get it to happen in a bungalow because you can't get the coffin in or out of it. You're not going to bring a corpse out of doors and put him in a coffin—you can't do that—It got to be done in the house. But I guess there's some of them you can do it. A lot of those bungalows—they have partitions and doors laid out every how. If I lived in this house a lifetime, I'd like to be waked here. That's the way it was done—every old man, every Irishman or Irishwoman was ever here they were all waken in their own homes—Carried to the church—they'd toll the bell at the start of the funeral. They'd walk around shore in the summer, the funeral—string of people would reach from here to Cluett's Height—farther than that, halfway around shore.

BEN FOLEY ON WAKES: That was a great fray then, boy—stay up all night then, eight or nine people stay up all night—have all kinds of fun at a wake!

The second-floor hallway of Harold Dwyer's house

"tangle" of the harbor, as witnessed by the recent construction of houses along the road to Sandy Cove. Locating a house away from the community indicates a change from relying on family and neighbors to independence and privacy, but some builders are forced into this situation because suitable land for constructing a new house is not available in the harbor.[13] Many residents of new houses still construct new outbuildings or use existing outbuildings, and many continue to keep animals, cut their own wood, and maintain their gardens.

The layout of Tilting's houses affects its residents' visiting. In Tilting's older houses, neighbors entering the house through the back door had direct access to the kitchen and indirect access to "the room." Strangers and special visitors had fairly direct access to "the room" when they entered the front door, but they may not have been invited to come into the kitchen. While at first glance the plan of the new bungalow or split-level may appear to be "open" in character compared to hall and parlor– or center hall–plan houses, the use and size of the rooms in the new houses were different. They were single-purpose rooms that worked against quick, informal visits, wakes, and dancing. Visiting in new houses requires removing your boots so the wall-to-wall carpeting will not be spoiled, and settling in a friend's living room is not as straightforward as squatting in an old kitchen. In the old house, all informal activities took place in the kitchen, and there was an air of informality and congeniality. Furniture was easy to move to accommodate these activities, and in winter everyone gathered there around the wood stove.

The old house was open to visiting because the occupants were focused outward. Visitors were always anticipated: waiting for someone to come down the lane, to enter the house to share news about the community or family, about the success of a fishing or hunting trip, the weather, or strangers visiting the harbor. This everyday news connected the residents with each other and their surroundings, and often carried with it the possibility of taking immediate action to help someone in need. Fergus Burke told me his father never missed a night without "going on a cruise," his father's generation's way of saying "going for a visit."

FERGUS BURKE ON BUNGALOWS:
They were supposed to be terrible damp, bungalows or one-story houses. They were, too. They didn't have enough of heat, see?

Top: New houses by Allan and Mary Keefe's house and fishing stage
Bottom: Old and new houses around the harbor, viewed from Bunker Hill

ANNIE FOLEY ON VISITING: You'd never be ashamed to go in. Wherever you went in, you'd be welcome. Sit down around, sing songs. We used to sing a lot. I used to sing, and my sister Elsie used to sing, and when we'd go into a house, well, there'd be a crowd of men sitting down, the wife would be there, and the husband, and they'd say, "Oh look! The Reardon girl is coming—we'll have some songs then." No trouble to get us to sing. No music then or anything like that. We'd start in and sing—all the girls used to sing then. Everybody would sing in their turn, men and women, right around the house. That was our way of living then. Everybody was so happy then, it wasn't even funny. Nobody's happy now—we got everything.

During my first winter in Tilting, children from the neighborhood would frequently come into my kitchen without knocking and sit down, often without saying a word. Curious about my drawing board and instruments, they would watch me for a while and then leave as quietly as they came in. Visiting without formalities like knocking on the door is still common in Tilting and elsewhere in Newfoundland. But the older residents of Tilting feel the style of visiting they once knew, which had much in common with the ceili in Ireland, is disappearing.[14]

Weather requiring boots persists for much of the year in Tilting. Residents are familiar with the rules for removing footwear for each house in the community, and an attitude toward visiting is expressed in these rules. Older residents tend to admonish visitors in a friendly way to come in without taking off their boots. At one time, there was no need to remove your footwear on a short visit; the visit would be confined to the kitchen where the floor was mopped several times daily. Clarence Foley told me visitors never went further than the kitchen unless a wake was held in the parlor.

The different ways of heating old and new houses also affects visiting. Only one room is heated in the old house, usually the kitchen (either the inside kitchen or the back kitchen).[15] Visiting cannot easily be separated from the daily activities of the kitchen. The wood or oil

ON MUMMERS

JIM GREENE: I believe it was twelve of them. They'd rap at the door first, and once the door was open—the woman or someone would open the door, they'd introduce themselves and she'd say, "Come in"—he'd come in and say what he had to say and sit down and the door was still open, they'd all come in until they were all in and full the house! They'd come in the kitchen. No one would say a word while they were all coming in—they'd talk to the people after they got in and they'd have a drink then—all them fellows had a bottle of rum—rum they used to drink. You'd never know who they were, unless you had an idea before and heard about from one to the other—you'd never know who the hell they were, unless you knew from their size or bulk. They'd stay the whole day in the one house—drinkin' and singin' and everything—that night they'd move on to the next house. But they wouldn't go into every house, you know, that's another thing about them—they knew the house that they were going to be alright in, and knew where they were going to get something to eat—there was only the one group of mummers in the whole community.

ANNIE FOLEY: They used to have rhymes, the mummer rhymes. That was a real organization to itself. They would practice that for months and months before ever Christmas came around. That was the real olden days!

CLARENCE FOLEY: They were dressed up grand.

BEN AND ANNIE FOLEY ON VISITING:

[Ben] The reason people would be embarrassed was because they didn't have much to eat. [Annie] Where you go in now they got salt meat, eggs, or ham, or bacon or something. People were different then, there was people in the world wouldn't eat before you, before strangers. If anyone came in and you were eating you would knock.

cast-iron stove, placed in a prominent position in the center of the house, is a focus for visitors. The stove and its large teakettle is an obvious sign of welcome. During the course of a visit, the performance of the stove is a frequent and seemingly inexhaustible topic for conversation. It is anything but a passive appliance, requiring stoking and frequent adjustments. Stovetops and teakettles are frequently and lovingly cleaned and polished, and over the years they take on an elegant patina.

Dorothy Burke said at one time people were always waked in their own homes. Wakes lasted for two nights, and candles were burned day and night. Everyone in the harbor would visit at all hours, and they always would be offered food provided by neighbors. After the corpse was washed and laid out, the husband or wife would sit in the rocking chair next to the deceased for two days, dressed in black.

Edith Reardon told me the window blinds of the house would be closed for twelve months in the case of the death of a close relative. In the kitchen the blinds would be only half down. In all Tilting's old houses, the windows had both cotton blinds and lace curtains. If a neighbor died, the blinds in every house would be down until burial day. When the funeral procession passed a house, the blinds had to be put down.[16] This custom stopped in the 1970s. Edith's parents were waked in their own house, in the parlor, head to the west, feet to the east. There was never anyone special in the community to prepare the dead as friends and neighbors always performed this task. After waking at home died out, wakes were held in the church. The first funeral home on Fogo Island opened in 1987 near Barr'd Islands.

Jack Reardon's house in Sandy Cove, the last house remaining in this cove after resettlement to Tilting. Fishing nets are drying on the ground around the house, and the grass is short from grazing animals.

Dan Greene said waking often took place in the kitchen, sometimes even in the back kitchen: "People used to have their coffin ready before they died a long time ago. Many people had their lumber for their coffin put away—wide, rough boards." Clarence Foley told me, "There'd be none of this thousand dollar casket—we'd make them and cover them with mounting—just as nice as those bought ones. That would be just as nice—just as good—all for about thirty or forty dollars. There was a fellow here one time—he come from Boston—he said, 'It's a cheap place to die.'"

BEN FOLEY ON VISITING:
Today, there be no one to come in.

In '33 I came home from Boston. I went in the woods that year and cut some of the framing. I built the house meself—no help whatsoever, only the fellows come and help me to shingle it—no help whatsoever, nobody never done nothing. And I put the rafters up on it meself— I upped the rafters out there on the cliff, and 'twas a fine day and I had to get them up there—and all the guys gone in the woods—I wanted two fellows anyway to help me do it— they're big and heavy. When the fellows come out of the woods I had all the rafters on meself—I had them locked, all ready to go up—and I put up big beams, one over here and one over there, and I put two ropes on each end of it and I slide them up on the beams—heavy work. I got the wood on this island, on Fogo Island—right across on the other side of the island—fir and spruce—mostly fir—sills, sleepers, everything cut on the island. They're great big sticks—two flats on them, that's all, and I put them up same as they were cut—I left them big in the butt. All the sashes, made 'em myself—glazed 'em myself. I made them doors meself. And all them door frames, I went in on the island and cut the sticks and sawed them with the pit saw and they're all plowed out—all the one piece, these door jams. Any other house you go in, you'll see just the two-by-four nailed up and the facing nailed on it.

CHAPTER 3

BUILDING AND LAUNCHING THE HOUSE

-- -- -- -- -- -- -- -- -- -- --

I *AM SITTING IN JIM GREENE'S* kitchen on a cold winter's day. We just met for the first time, although he has heard of a stranger in the harbor "scourging" people with questions about old houses. I awkwardly explain the purpose of my visit. Jim gracefully agrees to teach me about house construction according to the traditional techniques used for generations by house builders in Tilting. He tells me most of the old houses in Tilting are about sixteen by twenty-four feet in plan, and about twelve feet high on the post (corner post height). These are the three critical dimensions needed for their layout and construction. Jim always made roofs on houses he constructed "a square" (forty-five-degree pitch). He made his house, constructed in 1934 to 1935, nineteen and a half feet wide and twenty-four feet long with a height on the post of twelve and a half feet. He wanted his house fairly low for wind protection, and he wanted it to have a unique design. Other men from Tilting would often come by to look at his house during construction, and his house influenced the design of two other houses in the community.

Construction started by placing one heavy "squared" (rectangular) wooden sill (six by six inches or preferably larger) on top of blocks.[1] The rest of the sills were put down in relation to the first one, and the corners were notched and lapped for extra strength. Then spruce shores were placed under the sills, and the sills were leveled. The shores could be left in the round not only to save time but for greater strength. If you could get them, salt water logs (drift wood like old pit props found along the sea shore) or old, preserved wharf sticks were best for shores. A shoulder was cut on the shores, about two and a half inches wide. The shores were then spiked in to the sills with four-inch nails. Diagonal shores, called dagger shores, were also used to stabilize the house foundation. These were placed at a pronounced angle, with two on each gable end sill, and three on each side sill, the longer the better. Spruce was used for these dagger shores, and dagger-shore anchors also had to be provided, either by using a notch in the bedrock or by placing

Jim Greene's house, which he built himself when he returned from Boston

Ed McGrath's house during demolition

Second-floor stair guard detail

Stair and wall detail

House eave detail

House floor beam layout

the shore against something solid. Often builders boarded in the space under the bottom of the house with clapboards attached to a flared wood frame that projected down and out from the sills to the ground. The flare of the clapboard skirt made the foundation appear neater and stronger, and kept animals like sheep from sheltering under the house. These clapboarded skirts were often painted a different color than the main part of the house, and they were carefully fitted around the irregular, projecting profile of bedrock under the house.

Sleepers or floor beams were placed between sills, wedged into place with an angled notch cut in the sill and a matching angled profile for the end of the sleeper. Jim once found in a floor beam a bullet that had lodged in the tree when the tree was young. The sleepers were spiked to the sill with a six-inch spike or trenail. A middle sill was placed under the sleepers for extra support. Then "uprights" (exterior wall studs) were installed on top of the sills, toenailed in place. These uprights were four inches thick, and at this point in the construction they could be any length because they were cut off later. The front and back walls were constructed first, then the gable-end walls. Next the first floor was put down. This consisted of two layers of tongue-and-groove boards with a layer of birch bark in between, providing extra protection against drafts and a robust floor for heavy first-floor loads.

The next phase of construction involved attaching "girts" or ledgers to the inside face of the uprights. These extended the full length

Notched sill floor construction detail (left) and carriage beam support detail (right) at Ed McGrath's house

JIM GREENE SHOWING ME HIS HOUSE: Now, you asked to see the house you can see it—this is where the kids plays—just a livin' room—where we goes in and watches TV and has a drink of beer or—somebody comes in wants to see us, that's all. Now then, I had to get these stairs in—see? Now, all this stuff, I made this myself—all those rods, I made all them myself—I made the lathe meself—a foot-powered lathe with a pole up there on the beams and a line on it—now, everything had to work out—this step had to be the same as the bottom one. See this? (curved return of stair railing at the top of the stair)—I can take you in the woods on the middle of the island and show you where I cut that thing—I was walking along and I knew I wanted this—I'd have to cut it out of a wide board and if I do, it would be cross-grained and break—wouldn't it? That round thing there is a Juniper—it's good for a thousand years.

of the house just below the level of the second-floor beams, which rested on top of the girts. Sometimes extra support was needed for the mantelpiece, the heavy beam near the exterior wall of the kitchen that supported the brick chimney for the wood stove. Jim remembers a house in Deep Bay, Fogo Island, which had extremely large wooden knees (naturally formed L-shaped tree trunks, turned upside down) supporting the mantelpiece. These extended two feet horizontally and five feet vertically, and they were exposed on the interior of the kitchen. Later these knees were taken from the house and recycled to support a boat deck. Some mantelpieces were very large, up to twelve inches square.

After the uprights were plumbed in place, the two-by-four wall plate was "cracked" (fitted) on top of the uprights. Then "couples" (rafters) were prepared. The couples were first "locked" (joined at the peak) in place by laying them flat on the first floor, which was the easiest place to work. A centerline was marked on the floor to assist with locking the couples, and either a butt joint (toenailed) or lapped joint (four-inch spike) could be used. Then the second-floor beams were installed, and these could be used as a scaffold to stand on for installing the couples. Couples were placed against the long, gable-end wall uprights, and the uprights were marked and cut off. The couples were placed on top of the trimmed gable-end uprights and spiked

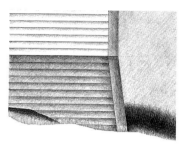

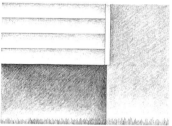

Top: A foundation detail with wooden shores on an old house. The connection between the foundation structure and the ground was tenuous but congenial and accepted topographical irregularities.
Bottom: The concrete foundation detail of a new house, constructed with heavy equipment on a leveled site.

and toenailed in place. If an upright was too short, another could be placed alongside it and spiked into place. After this the other gable-end couples were installed, then the middle couples.

The final stage of construction was to make the house "watertight" (closed in). First came exterior-wall sheathing, roof sheathing, then roof shingles, windows and doors, clapboard, and paint. The brick chimney was done last. According to Jim roofs were all different pitches: flat, halfway, and square. Flat (low-pitched) roofs required the use of felt, which was first used in Tilting around 1905. Before this all roofs were steep-pitched gable roofs with wood shingles. Wood shingles of fir and spruce were manufactured in Carmanville[2] and also in Southern Arm, Birchy Bay. Sometimes these shingles were green and were installed close together. If they were dry, you had to leave a space or they would "buff up" (warp). They came in eighteen-inch lengths and all different widths: six, seven, eight, even two inches. Single-ply felt was sometimes used under wood shingles, but often birch rind or no underlay was used. Jim said that Fred Greene's house had birch rind under the shingles: these shingles were good forever and would never rot. An old carpenter from Noggin Cove told Jim the best way to sheath the roof is with four-inch boards, eliminating every other board and exposing part of the wood shingles in the attic so the shingles can breathe.

Wood shingles had to be painted with a mixture of cod liver oil and ochre, which would make them the color of dried blood. Some people used to paint them gray, and others would tar them black. Jim feels the best treatment is cod liver oil and ochre, applied every two or three years. A ridge board was placed at the peak of the roof, sometimes painted white. Flashing extended over a bed of mortar that bridged the gap between the chimney and the roof framing.[3]

Window sashes were locally made, but not everyone could make them. Solomon Saunders in Cape Cove was known as an expert sash maker. He also made violins and played them, and he made his own wooden planes and even an auger. The sashes were made with hand planes, chisels, and a lock saw. A common window glass size was eight by ten inches for the old style of multipane windows (nine-pane or twelve-pane windows). Later glass sizes were ten by twelve inches, then twelve by eighteen inches, and they cost ten cents per pane in the 1930s.

All the larger-dimension pine in the old houses was pit-sawn by hand. Interior wall partitions were always vertical single-board partitions made from tongue-and-groove boards and sometimes notched into the side walls. The old gable-roof houses had coped ceilings, but people started to do away with the cope in the early 1900s: they wanted "square lofts" (higher ceilings at the perimeter of the second floor). Jim feels the coped ceiling makes the house stronger. To make a coped ceiling, collar beams were nailed into the sides of the roof couples, and these beams supported the attic floor. For the exterior cladding, Jim was

MARTIN GREENE ON THE HOUSE HIS FATHER, LAMBERT, BUILT:

They couldn't get over there was that many windows in it. Thought we had too many windows. But the windows was just right. Lambert placed the windows where he wanted them and everything laid out. He never changed no more. I never changed them meself. 'Twas right already—we lived there down below the road. He bought an old one alongside of Mike Greene's—so we launched that over and we lived in that until we got this one built—a few year—and we went to work and we built this one.

We'd coat them wood shingles—we'd render out the oil, the liver, fish liver, and we'd get about fifteen or twenty pound of ochre, and boil it for a couple of days in a drum, and heave in about a half a gallon of red paint—and let it boil and stir it. The same thing applies to my stable out there. You'll still get the ochre. You get your red ochre and your cod oil, my son, I guarantee it—it'll go right through the clapboard, my son. Our premises, our stable and our stages now—I guarantee you we kept them up—with the red ochre and the white trimmings. They used to be worth looking at—guarantee you, worth looking at! I liked the red—we used to go in for the red—the windows and all that, we used to have that red you see, and the clapboard white. Now Alonze's, his house was painted yellow, you see, and he had the white trim—it didn't show up like the red, see? I didn't fancy it. 'Twas what they used to call this buff paint, 'twas right yellow, you see, and he used to have the white trim—and 'twas nearly all the one color, only a little difference. But the red and the white, boy—it really showed.

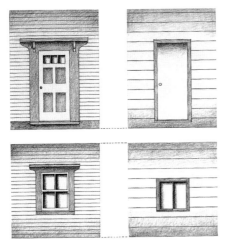

Left: Original (left) and renovated (right) trim and fenestration on an old house in Tilting. The renovation portrays a less friendly, "intensive" character as opposed to the original "extensive" and welcoming trim.
Right: The front of the Kinsella house on The Rock

also aware of how rain screens equalize air pressure. This state-of-the-art detail is used in present-day house construction. It provides a cross-ventilated air space under the clapboards that is open to the outside air, and this helps to eliminate leaks from wind-driven rain (air pressure is equalized on both sides of the exterior cladding). Jim said the warmest houses had clapboards directly on the uprights with no sheathing and no building paper so the wind could go out. Although this is not the detail that would be used in house construction today, the general principle is the same.

Jim Greene's account of basic house construction ended there, but much more work still had to be done to finish the house. In addition to constructing stairs and guardrails, interior trim and wallpaper had to be installed, and panel doors and furniture had to be made. Charlie Lane told me people were trying to convince him to install modern hollow-core doors in his old house to replace his old mortise and tenon–panel doors, but he resisted: "I wouldn't get rid of the doors— they're handmade."

Like Tilting's boats, its houses had to be detailed to guard against wet conditions and salt from the sea spray. Building on an exposed seacoast was made even worse by wind, rain, snow, ice storms, fog, and dampness; houses had only a very short season to dry out. The weather made it hard to keep the paint on the house, and the old square nails used for trim and clapboards would quickly rust.

The proportions of materials, windows and doors, and trim played a major role in the appearance and scale of Tilting's older houses. The difference between these carefully proportioned, locally made traditional architectural elements and today's purchased construction components becomes painfully apparent when old houses are improperly renovated. The Kinsella house achieved a congenial effect by using narrow clapboards, wide trim boards, and windows with true divided window-panes. When instead narrow, painted wood clapboards are replaced by wide vinyl or aluminum siding, locally made wood windows by factory-made vinyl sliding windows, and the locally made, paneled front door with projecting, bracket-supported canopy by a slab door with minimal trim, the house appears less open to visitors and to the outside world.

Frank Mahoney's front door still had its original trim into the late 1980s. His house was the only house in Tilting with a dormer window. A clever use of trim boards can create the impression that a house is larger than it really is. In most hall-and-parlor houses in Tilting, a vertical trim board was placed in the middle of the facade to provide a third compositional element for the front of the house. This gave the house a more monumental appearance, almost as if it had more than one structural bay. The Cluett house on The Rock creates such a grand effect of multiple structural bays.[4] The wood trim on the facade combined with diagonal clapboards and colored glass windows high-light the status of the house, which once belonged to the Bryan family. The trim on the Cluett house is similar to the trim found on many lodge buildings (men's service clubs) in other communities in Newfoundland. On the Foley house's corner trim board detail, layers of wood trim were built up, adding substance to the appearance of the corner by creating multiple shadow lines. This detail matches the corner detailing of some of Tilting's locally made furniture.

Above: The front elevation of a typical hall-and-parlor house. The center trim board creates the impression of an additional structural bay and represents a third element in the tripartite, bilaterally symmetrical composition of the façade.

Opposite: Frank Mahoney sitting in front of his house. After he retired from fishing, he often sat here await-ing the return of Tilting's fishing boats. He could predict the success of a fishing trip from the displacement of the boat in the water.

The front facade of the house in Tilting was so important that it was sometimes the only outside wall painted. The sides and the back of the house were stained with red ochre, matching the small outbuildings behind the house.[5] This was a way of economizing when funds did not permit the entire house to be painted.

The traditional wooden gutter was an important architectural element on Tilting's old houses. The gutter on Albert and Philomena Cluett's stable was once used to collect rainwater in a puncheon, since they could not have a well on their premises. For drinking water the Cluetts had to haul water from a well off their premises or from Sandy Cove Pond. Wooden gutters like the Cluetts' require care in their detailing and construction, as in the notched gutter detail that elegantly turns the corner. Rather than install a modern ready-made metal or vinyl gutter with downspout that hides the flow of water, the Cluetts chose to

keep their traditional wooden gutter. In materials, scale, and color, the wooden gutter harmonizes with the rest of the exterior trim of the stable.

Dan Greene described the wooden gutter on his house. He collected rainwater from his back-kitchen roof because his well would go dry in summer. Dan made the wooden chutes himself, using boards he bought from Earle's, and these overlapped and were attached by cleats to the roof eaves. A tierce was placed under the end of the chute, and a line was tacked in the end of the chute to the tierce to keep wind from blowing the water stream away from the tierce. "Boy, it was the grandest water—good for washing."

When I first started my fieldwork in Tilting, I assumed aerial photography would help me to document house placement and ownership. However, the earliest aerial photograph from 1949 showed me that many of the existing houses and outbuildings were not where they were supposed to be. I later learned that the older houses and outbuildings were designed and built for mobility. They were often moved or "launched," either when they were sold or when they were relocated to a more convenient site. When a house was sold in Tilting, the land was rarely included in the sale. This required moving the house to another location.

In Tilting people were used to launching heavy boats like bully boats and schooners, and the connection with house launching is obvious. Houses were placed on heavy, purpose-built wooden sleds, which were then pulled either by men or by horses across the ice of the harbor. Houses were also floated across open water (pulled by a small boat like a trap skiff). Recently, a few houses have been moved by tractor on the road. Some houses were moved two or three times, and a few were moved to other communities. One house was moved to another site but was later returned to its original site. Greg Reardon recalled two houses in the Gulch that were moved twice, and both times together.[6] Additions like back kitchens were removed before a house was launched. As in the Reardon house, many older houses had small masonry chimneys for wood stoves that were supported by a heavy wood beam

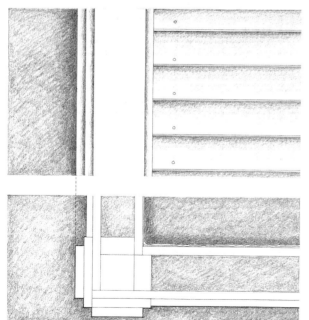

Top left: *Albert and Philomena Cluett's house on The Rock. The Cluetts purchased the house when they moved from Cape Cove to Tilting.*
Top right: *Detail of the front of the Cluett's house*
Bottom left: *A corner trim board detail from Philomena and Clarence Foley's house on The Rock. Layers were built up with wood trim, adding substance to the appearance of the corner by creating multiple shadow lines.*
Bottom right: *A wooden gutter on Albert Cluett's stable, used to collect rainwater for washing*

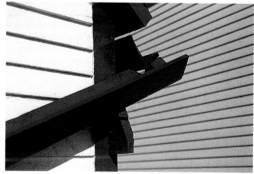

FRANK MAHONEY ON HOUSE LAUNCHING: Oh, my son, you didn't have to ask anybody. All they had to do was put the two spars under it and say you were ready and they wouldn't stop till they put it right where you were going to put it.

Men preparing to "launch" a house in Tilting using levers to lift the house (photo circa 1950 by Father J. M. O'Brien, courtesy Clara Byrne)

in the first-floor ceiling. The chimney could easily be removed for house launching and rebuilt in the new location.[7] According to Frank Mahoney, the chimney in his son's house was not removed before launching, and they even left furniture in the house while it was being moved. "Gary's house come from over by Anthony Foley's and the dishes were on the table—never stirred."

A few houses, like Richard Walsh's house on The Rock, were dismantled in sections and re-erected on new sites in Tilting. Rose Burke's house originally faced the harbor but was turned on its site to face people entering the community by road. Dan Greene described renovations to Austin Foley's house, built around 1890. Instead of turning the house around, the stair was turned and the windows were reversed from front to back, again so the house could face the road. Ned Cluett's house was floated up to Tilting from Cape Cove after the chimney was removed.[8]

Ben Foley told me the story of launching his house on March 11, 1942. The back kitchen was removed first, and the house was placed on a house-launching sled. This was made from heavy wooden beams called "skids," with timber cross bars attached with trenails. It was too slippery for the men to haul the house on the ice at first ("as slippery as glass"), so they tried to haul the house with eleven horses.

JIM GREENE ON THE LAST HOUSE HE LAUNCHED:
Oh, my—the last house I launched here was for Ed
Healey—we got a tractor to haul it. You bolt a piece
across the back and the front of the house on top of
your runners. When you turn in the road you're going
to twist, and when you twist, you'll haul the runner
underneath it—but if you got one beam down
between the two runners, one runner's shoving the
other and you can't do it [haul the runner underneath
it]—they had plenty of trouble that way—and then
you put a wire strap around it—and bore holes down
through here and come around the house and put
those big wire straps through in the center like a bridle
with big shackles in them—the tractor come on,
shackle onto this, and go on.

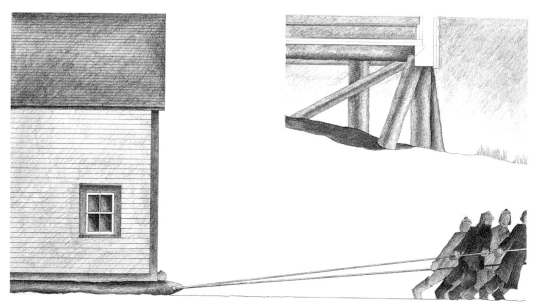

A typical wood foundation detail using wooden shores and diagonal "dagger" shores, and house
launching using a sled pulled by men

JIM GREENE ON HOUSE LAUNCHING: Most houses, if there was a chimney in them, they took them down. Well, you talkin' about me and how I did this house, my brain must have been alright 'cause nearly every house in this harbor's after being launched, and you know, they used to come to me to launch them houses? I can go out and point out all around the harbor houses that I launched. The first thing you got to get it off the foundation—got to get the runners underneath it—the big sticks that it's hauled on—and you wants to know how to do that. You wants to know how to rig out that house—put it in a—I'd say it's a sled. I must have launched twenty houses. There was no foreman, maybe two hundred men there, and you'd have trouble sometimes—and you knows how to get out of that trouble, what to do—where to put the sticks. We raised it up with prises—you know what they are? You get five, ten, twenty men, however many men you got—come down on this, and up she goes—no trouble—twice as fast as you'll do it with a jack—but you'll want the men. Then you block it—you shove in blocks right around it. There's a trick in putting it up—you knock out all the blocks except the center blocks and the house swings itself—it don't take no power. Put the blocks in the center so the weight of the house helps you put it up—same thing with hauling up a boat—it's balanced—no trouble. After you get it up, then you shove your great big runners through—the biggest kind of sticks, you'd have to go off the island for them. At that time we used to have lots of big schooners here and those spars they'd take out would be the right thing— but now, there's none of them—they got to go in on the mainland and they cost like the devil. Once I went through the ice, but it wasn't too bad. But another fellow, they broke right through, right down to the roof of the house—they left it there and they worked at it and sawed all the ice out in the pond ahead out toward where they were going and went in the cove down there and sawed the ice and made a channel for it, and when the water'd rise they hauled it on in on the land. The paper spoiled—it spoiled all that but the house never hurted—it done it good. Len Broders is living in the house down there now.

Unfortunately, they broke through the ice in Peter's Cove. The next day men were able to get the house up on the land and they hauled it to its present site. The Foleys waited until May to place the foundation shores, and until June to reattach the back kitchen.

Allan Keefe told me that the best time for launching a house over the ice was the latter part of March. The men would stop for a spell halfway across the ice. Fergus Burke told me that before people started to use horses in Tilting, manpower was used. Every man in the harbor was invited to a house launching.

At various times in Tilting's history, there was a surplus of houses, and so it is not surprising that houses were moved. House launching demonstrates the community's connection with its past by reusing an old house rather than demolishing it. Perhaps more importantly, house launching ensured that land, always scarce around the harbor, would remain in the family. In contrast to Tilting's old houses, new houses are not mobile. They are placed on concrete foundations that change the landscape, usually requiring the use of heavy excavating equipment. When these new houses are sold, the land is sold with the house.

JIM GREENE ON HOUSE LAUNCHING: Before horses they used manpower—maybe seventy-five to eighty men—that'd have to be snow and ice—you wouldn't haul it on the ground on the bare gravel, no—and they used to use horses too, but them horses wouldn't work. If you could get them working all together it would be good. You'd take them houses across the ice of the harbor if you can. You come in a cove somewhere—you pick out a level place where you can come in, maybe a couple of hundred yards further than you'd have to go, that's the place where you'd have to come in where 'twas level.

I suppose I got a bad fashion—I never answers a knock—knock comes to the door I sings out, "Come on in, boy!" you see? I never answer the door but you should. I don't like it—go and meet the fellow in the door and turn him away. I never turn anyone away from the door yet—they're not going to come for me—I knows that—not going to do me any harm, you see? Say if the Jehovah's Witness comes and they got their papers—Well, all I got to do is say I'm not interested in your religion, I got me own and I'm going to follow it up till I dies and no one going to change me over and that's what me mother and father reared me up at—and then perhaps they'd say would you want a paper and I'd say yes 'cause they're not going to—I wouldn't ignore him. Sure, I could put it in the stove after he's gone if I like—we're all humans.

CHAPTER 4

INSIDE THE HOUSE

----

*I*T TOOK ME A WHILE to get comfortable with Tilting's custom of entering houses without knocking. Today you can still walk right in if you are known in the community, but it is important to become familiar with signals from the occupants that it may be an inconvenient time for a visit. After a while people get to know the signals of a particular house. If privacy is desired in the evening, the porch light may be off, the window blinds drawn, and the lights turned off downstairs. To indicate no one is home, a mop and pail or broom may be placed against the back door, or the gate may be barred.[1] I heard of one resident who was able to reach around and place the mop and pail against the exterior of the back door while remaining inside in order to indicate no one was at home. At one time the absence of smoke coming from the chimney carried the same message.

Once inside you will find that Tilting's old houses used their rooms like houses in other rural Newfoundland communities did. The kitchen was a quasi-public room and the center of visiting and daily life, and was sometimes used as a work room. Fergus Burke remembers that Ed McGrath would mend his fishing nets in his kitchen in the spring of the year because it was warmer for working. The living room (called "the room") was reserved for the rare occasion of formal visiting, and it was a place where family photographs and treasures were displayed. Usually, only someone who was ill would use a bedroom during the day. As Pearce Dwyer told me, the proper place for a nap was on the kitchen couch. Living room couches in new houses are too soft and precious for someone taking a quick nap with work clothes on. For this you needed a kitchen couch, not too comfortable to ensure the nap was short, and also easy to clean. Dan Greene told me when he used to come in from fishing late at night in the summer and had to get up early the next morning, "Often you'd lie on the settle in your clothes. If you slept in a soft feather bed you couldn't get up. You had to lie on something hard." Going upstairs to the bedroom "meant you are more or less committed to the whole night."

Gladys McGrath in her kitchen with Amy and Jill McGrath. Gladys's kitchen is the central location for visiting in her neighborhood. Her house is surrounded by many of her sons' houses (Leo's, Frank's, Len's, Cyril's, and Andrew's) and the houses of close relatives.

Back kitchen additions were used as entrances to many of Tilting's houses, and usually had small porches to reduce drafts. They reduced the utility of the old, original kitchen and turned it into a larger type of living room. Another stove would be added to the back kitchen, making the back kitchen the new center of life in the house.

When I visit Dorothy Burke in her kitchen on Greene's Point, she is usually knitting next to her highly polished stove with the kettle on to boil. Dorothy prefers living on her side of the harbor. She likes the privacy of Greene's Point ("less people know what you are about") and the view of the harbor, and she thinks the other side of the harbor is too hot in summer. Fergus Burke told me kitchens were always placed on the south end of the house if possible, and Dorothy's kitchen fits this pattern.

In the house in which Pearce Dwyer grew up, people were always very busy, and the center of activity was the kitchen. In his kitchen there was no privacy, although there were usually only three or four people there at one time. It seemed to Pearce that he was always under-foot in the kitchen. But somehow things got done, all the cooking and cleaning up: "You were right in the middle of it." To get away from the tangle in the kitchen, he would sometimes go upstairs to read in bed. "The room" in his house was not used for sitting. Pearce's father, Fergus Dwyer, was waked in "the room." Some people had "balls, dinners, and dances" in their houses when Pearce was growing up, but he said the priest put an end to these "house rackets," and the custom ceased. For these parties the hosts would hold a duck "scoff" (a "big feed"), or a mutton supper.[2]

Center-hall houses had pantries on the first floor. In Pearce's house the pantry stored bulk food and was accessed from a small door

FRANK MAHONEY ON BACK KITCHENS: We used to live in this back kitchen—never looked in the main kitchen at all. 'Twas big enough for the family, and there was no need of us going in there unless we was going to bed. Always had the fire in here—never went out. We burned out a dozen comforts [stoves].

TED BURKE ON HOUSE LAYOUTS: Same thing, boy, the same thing. Laid out about the same, the same size—some with the stair in the center, more with stairs now in the end like this—well, they were laid out every how—that was the right way to say it. No fireplaces—they had the old-fashioned stoves. Some were big, some were small—it's all according to the wages they were getting then, you see. They'd always build on—that's the way it was—they'd put down a small house at first, for a young couple they got married—when they'd start rearing children then they'd gradually build on.

under the central stair. Christine Broders told me she used her pantry as a milk house. Alice Greene sometimes used her pantry in the same way, with shelves for milk, a table with butter on it, and basins for washing. Frank Mahoney said his pantry was used for bulk food, including pickled food like cabbage. Dorothy Burke used her "room" as a pantry in her house.

Fred Foley told me his parent's generation was very concerned about fire caused by wood stoves: "The old people hated fire—they never had a fire in the house at night. They would check to make sure there wasn't a spark in the stove about an hour after going to bed." But wood stoves were not the original method of heating in Tilting. Many senior residents I interviewed remembered open fireplaces in Tilting, or else they heard about open fireplaces from their parents. Greg and Bridget Reardon described the old Kehoe house in Tilting, which had an open fireplace made from field rocks and a wooden beam over the hearth opening. An iron crane was used to hang pots over the fire, and the family also made bread in pots. Walter Broders's house and Patrick Dwyer's house also had open fireplaces. Many senior residents told me that in the days of open fireplaces, before canvas mats became available, people used to scrub the board floors of their kitchens with sand from Sandy Cove beach and spruce boughs until the boards were bleached white. The uniform heat in the new house would have been considered unbearable to previous generations. People wore many layers of clothing and were outdoors a lot. When they visited, they made short visits to kitchens that were only tolerably warm.

Some families regularly served meals on a large platter (rather than individual plates), which was placed in the middle of the kitchen

Any one come here, like "strange," we'd go in there, in the inside room.

table for all to use. After supper, from October through the winter months, people would sit around the stove. Edith Reardon described a typical evening for her family when she was growing up. Her dad would sit on the couch, and her mom in her rocker. The children would sit on the floor on hooked mats. They would watch the flankers through the stove grate and listen to Edith's father sing. Sometimes they would have company in the evening, her parent's friends. The children were sent to bed if people came for tea. Gilbert Dwyer told me that in the early days, staying out late, after 11:00 P.M., was disgraceful.

Parents usually slept in one of the front bedrooms of the house. There was not much room for anyone, as Gertie Dwyer told me, "not enough room for two cats to fight." Furniture could quickly fill the rooms, so there were practical limitations on the quantity of it in the house. Many bedrooms were no longer than the exact length of a bed (beds were very short compared to present queen- and king-size standards). There were no closets. I asked Pearce Dwyer where people kept their clothes. He replied jokingly, "They never had any." But he admitted clothes were stored in "the room" in his family's old house. Chamber pots were essential bedroom items before the days of bathrooms and plumbing. It was just too cold to go outside to the outhouse in the middle of the night unless absolutely essential. Although some residents I interviewed did not care to remember the days of outhouse use in Tilting, they were in many ways more appropriate environmentally than the new septic systems that accompanied the installation of bathrooms in houses.[3]

Alice Greene described the interior of her house on Greene's Point. In her back kitchen, the walls originally had a wooden wainscot all around the room with wallpaper above the wainscot. When she renovated the back kitchen, she took down the wainscot and installed full-height wood paneling on the walls, where she hung holy pictures like "The Sacred Heart" and also pictures of her children. Before the back

Dorothy Burke in her kitchen on Greene's Point, the stove highly polished and the kettle on to boil. From the vantage point of her rocking chair, she can see who is coming to visit and who is going by on the road.

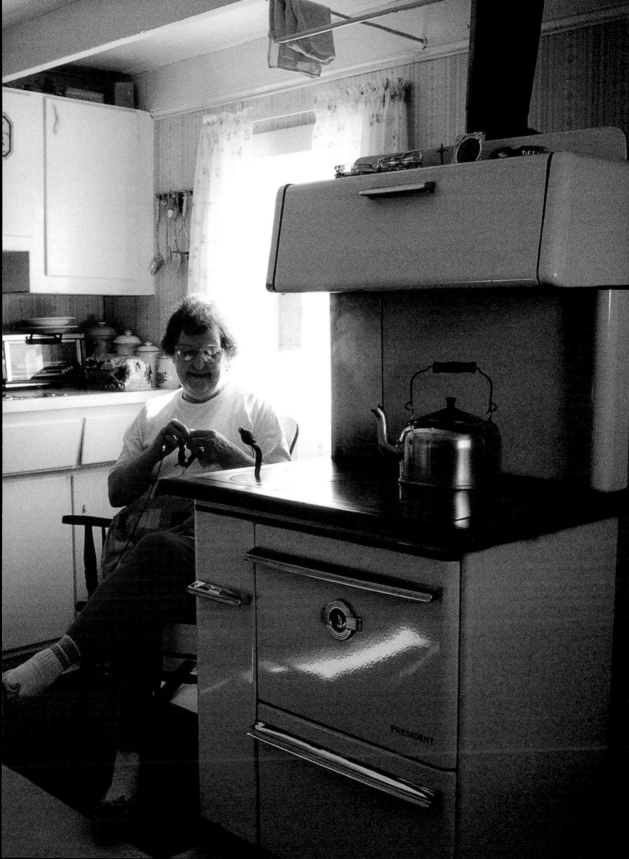

Most of them old houses then, they were all alike. They had the two couches, your table and your chairs, and your chiffonier, and that was it. They had the wood box in it—most every house had a wood box.

kitchen renovation, she had an old, locally made sideboard or "chiffonier" with dishes on top and one small shelf above, where she kept salt and pepper and other small items. She kept everyday dishes on the chiffonier, but pots, pans, and cutlery in closed cabinets or drawers. Her back kitchen also held two locally made couches or settles, a wooden table, a rocking chair, and a wood box. The stove she used was a "Comfort" brand stove with a square oven, and before that an "Improved Success" stove. When she renovated the back kitchen, she put the old couches outside in the garden for seating. The refrigerator replaced the rocking chair, and the new electric stove took up a lot of room. A daybed was moved into the back kitchen from the living room, and a basin was installed there for washing up after fishing. Built-in efficiency-type kitchen cabinets were installed in 1975.

On the walls of Alice's inside kitchen, she displayed consecration pictures with her children's names and photos. She still used the old inside kitchen as a kitchen, and had an oil range and a locally made cabinet with glass doors and shelves on top. These were made to fit on top of sideboards from about 1940 on. There was also a rocking chair, a chesterfield (a two-headed couch made by Alice's husband Herb), a daybed, and a wooden table. Above the table was an Aladdin lamp mounted on a bracket. The inside kitchen was used when the stove in the back kitchen smoked from a northerly wind or after the fall of the year. The back kitchen was closed down in winter; however, Herb would work there. Alice recalls, "He'd be out there singing away, repairing his nets."

Alice Greene's "room" had holy pictures and family pictures on the wall. The room was used as a children's study area and had a round table, Franklin heater, chairs, a davenport (which pulled out into a bed), and hooked mats on the floor. There was also an Aladdin lamp in the room and a kerosene lamp on the table. There was a chiffonier for glassware and special dishes; Alice told me that most houses had a chiffonier in the kitchen and also in the room.

The main bedroom in Alice's house had holy pictures and a crucifix, and also a sick call set, candles and other items that a priest would need for Last Rites. Alice told me that small holy shrines in houses went out of style about fifty years ago, but some families still used them. In Herb and Alice's bedroom there was a double iron bed with a feather mattress, a bureau with a mirror, and a washstand, commode, and chair. Clothes were hung in a garment bag. The children's bedrooms had a bed, a trunk for clothes, a bureau, and a mirror, but no washstand.

Alice described the typical meal schedule in her house. Breakfast was at 8:30 A.M., with pancakes, toast, eggs, and porridge. Dinner was served from 12:30–1:00 P.M. When her children were in school, they came home to eat, and this was their main meal. Supper was around 5:00 P.M., with a salad and leftovers. A snack, called a lunch, was served later in evening before bedtime.

Dorothy Burke described a similar schedule for her house, but with the addition of an afternoon snack around 3:30 P.M. She also told me about her family customs. Newborn babies were kept in a barracoat, a long flannel gown pinned up at the waistband. They used many quilts

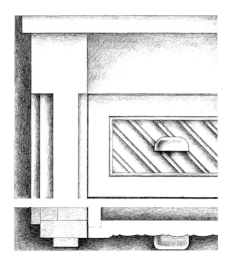

JIM GREENE ON FURNITURE MAKING:
I copied nothing—I just made the couch. I can show you one. There used to be one out in the store. I made this in '34, or '35—that was solid when it was made—upholstered with canvas, six or eight ounce duck—put it on, then paint it—you had to get a piece of cowhide for the edges. I made them legs meself.

A kitchen dresser in Martin Greene's house, with a corner trim detail similar to the corner trim boards on Philomena and Clarence Foley's house

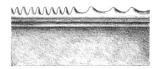

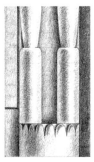

No, I never made no furniture—except tables and chairs—
and couches—I made two of them. I made some washstands—that washstand upstairs belonged to an old house
that my brother bought to get the land—and that old thing
was in it—and they threw it out and I was coming down
one day and they up there in the gulch—I see this, and
'twas all broken up—so I said, "That's a pity," and I took
this and I brought it in and nailed a piece of board across it
and asked my wife to paint it and there 'tis there.

in the crib, and the baby could hardly move. The baby drank milk
warmed over an oil lamp and on cold nights, it was placed in bed with
the parents. Cradles and swinging cots were used, and diapers were
washed by hand. Children took sponge baths in the kitchen, and adults
would have their baths in the kitchen in the evening after the children
were in bed. In the spring Dorothy's husband Louis would knit twine in
the kitchen every night. In summer the family ate their meals in the
back kitchen where it was cooler.

Compared to the rather restrained form of Tilting's houses, there
is a playful and exuberant quality in its furniture. This may be related
to the "spare time" (if there ever really was such a thing) winter activity
of furniture making for men (and sometimes women) and mat making
for women after all the exhausting chores were done. Like house
construction, furniture construction often used recycled materials, such
as packing crates.

Standard pieces like dressers and washstands were built in Tilting,
but not without imaginative design. Tilting's furniture makers were
influenced by commercial furniture catalogs, but local interpretations
often displayed exaggerated form. Furniture makers in Tilting felt free to
experiment with transformations and details that went beyond popular

Above: Ornamental carving is often present on Tilting's locally made furniture and picture frames

They'd have "chiffoniers" they used to
call them. You'd make them with two
drawers on top and two doors under and
a fancy back—perhaps a mirror in it.

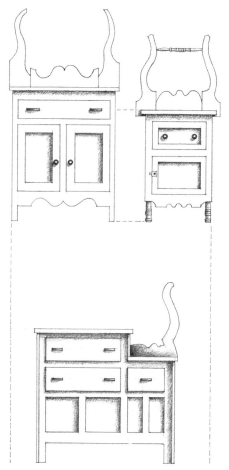

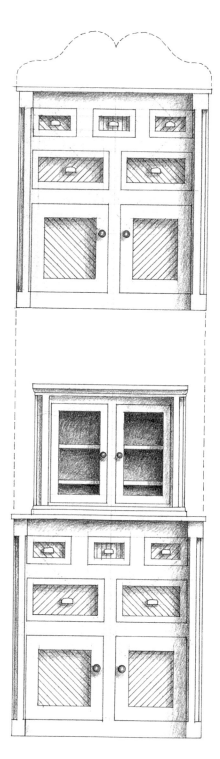

*Above: A bedroom dresser (top left) and a washstand (top right)
influenced the piece of furniture I found while walking one day
on Kelly's Island.*
Right: The chiffonier in Martin Greene's house

Oh, yes—anyone who could make it, you know—anyone who could make a piece of furniture they'd make it—and perhaps they'd sell it to someone who wanted a piece of furniture—a bureau or a washstand.

furniture styles. Furniture making offered unique possibilities for personal expression. Ornament was added to furniture edges by hand carving, and furniture surfaces could be "de-materialized" through false wood grains and paint patterns, adding another layer of form to the design.

Tilting's furniture can be described in three ways: evolutionary, hybrid, and reuse. The kitchen dresser in Martin Greene's house shows the first method. The curved back of the original piece was removed, and a glass cabinet was added. This gave the dresser, like many Tilting kitchen dressers (also known as sideboards or chiffoniers), three zones: a utilitarian, closed-in cabinet area below; a top surface for dishes for everyday use; and a small shelf projecting from the ornamental back-board to display fancy items.[4] The change from the open form of the kitchen dresser to the closed form of the kitchen cabinet occurred in the 1940s, when the old kitchen was displaced by a larger living room.

The second type of furniture method involves hybrid combinations. While walking one day on Kelly's Island, I found a piece of furniture discarded and broken on the rocks. I took a photograph, but I later realized I should have tried to save it. This was a strange piece of furniture, a hybrid, combined form that was apparently based on the basic design of a washstand and a dresser. This piece of furniture may forever remain a mystery.

The third type of furniture method results from reusing or recycling items made for another purpose, such as a flour-barrel rocking

Ted Burke with a small confirmation dresser with hand-carved edge and drawer ornament

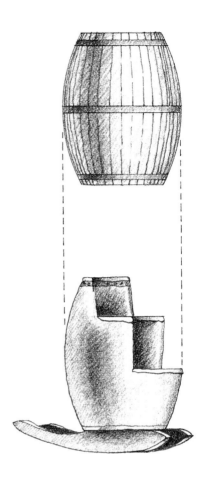

Lam Sandy lived in Cape and he used to varnish, and then he'd take the rabbit's paw, dip it down in the varnish, and do it right over—and he used to make his own violins, you know.

Top left: Flour barrels in the pantry of the Lane House Museum
Top right: Construction of flour-barrel rocking chair shown in the drawing
Left: This drawing shows Lambert Saunder's (Lam Sandy's) "secret" process for false wood graining

Left: A kitchen couch or "settle" made by John Kinsella. Dan Greene told me that when he used to come in from fishing late at night in the summer and had to get up early the next morning, "Often you'd lie on the settle in your clothes. If you slept in a soft feather bed you couldn't get up. You had to lie on something hard." Right: John Kinsella's carpentry tools and his tool chest. John made most of the furniture in his house.

chair. When upholstered and turned into chairs, flour barrels provide a surprisingly comfortable and snug fit, and they keep your back warm and free of drafts in winter.

Ornamental carving often decorates Tilting's locally made furniture and picture frames. Notching an edge with a pocket knife is similar to one of the most common ways to transform raw timber in Tilting— the rinding process used to strip the bark off wood before it can be used for fence pickets, beams, and stage or flake bedding.[5] Ted Burke gave me a small dresser made by Patrick Burke in the late 1800s. It was a child's Confirmation souvenir to keep odds and ends and small treasures. The edges and drawers are highly ornamented by ribbed carving patterns. Lambert Saunder (Lam Sandy), who lived in Cape Cove, was regularly contracted to do false wood graining on locally made furniture in Tilting. Everyone had to leave the room while he worked, and he used various "secret" items and techniques to work patterns into the varnish.

John Kinsella made most of the furniture in his house. He was the local Tilting agent for Earle Sons and Company of Fogo, and he lived next to these premises on The Rock.[6] For furniture making John had access to Earle's workshop until he retired. Val Kinsella's father, John, made the washstand and dresser in the bedroom of the second-floor addition to Val's house. Although the ceiling of the room is very low, it feels just right for someone lying down in bed. Just as rooms in the traditional Japanese house were not designed for the comfort of a person standing up, rooms in Tilting's houses seem to be designed for sitting or lying down.

Val Kinsella standing in the back bedroom, second-floor addition to the Kinsella house

Before linoleum or commercial floor-covering materials became available, small hooked mats were used to decorate and protect floors. In winter these were placed close together to help insulate the floor. They were cleaned for Christmas and put in the store in summer. Josephine Lidster remembered floors covered with painted sailcloth. Alice Greene told me Cecilia (Sis) Power[7] used to paint flowers on the canvas on her kitchen floor. When this pattern wore out, she would sometimes paint a diamond on the canvas. Annie Foley made mats throughout the winter, starting in December, usually on bad weather days. She would make rough patterns from other mats she admired. To copy another mat, she placed paper under the mat and used a darning needle to stab through the mat to make a perforated outline on the paper. Her friends would regularly visit to see her mats ("How many mats do you have now?"), and she would usually manage to make eight or ten mats each winter.

ROSE BURKE ON MATS: Sometimes you could buy a stamp mat. My mother would nearly always buy these—the pattern was stamped on it. "Brin" we used to call it. And, you'd work it in different colors—it was beautiful. And there were some people like Margie, Gerard's Margie—she could take her pen and pencil and put any kind of scrolls and everything on it. And you'd cut out the scrolls out of paper, you'd lay it down and mark it—that was the occupation night time, in the evenings when you'd get done with your work. Sometimes you'd make a hit-and-miss type of mat. I remember Saturdays I had to help. Take them out on the fence and beat them. Dirty things—and they used to scrub them then and take them to the cove—that was the last performance—take them and dip them up and down in the salt water, and that would bring out the color—how much they worked—how hard. Down home, my mother had great big mats. She'd spread them the whole length of the kitchen.

Left: Mat made by Catherine Kinsella, in the second-floor hallway of the Kinsella house
Opposite top: Mat made by Catherine Kinsella, now resting in its final destination in the fishing stage of the Kinsella premises
Opposite bottom: Mat made by Catherine Kinsella, at the top of the stairs in the house

The sun's coming out of the water—that's what we used to say. You can see it here—in May and in the first of June the sun will rise here, come up over the shoulder of the island, shine in through this window—and sets up here [Dan has sunrise and sunset of the longest and shortest day of the year marked on a wall in his house]. Before the sun would come up, a terrible red dawn would be there—just as red as to say everything's afire—the sun not up. I often be out there and the sun would come out of the water, red as blood—pure fire—and that's the day you'd get the northwest storm. You'd get in before it blew—if you didn't do that, you'd drive away, you couldn't row in.

CHAPTER 5

OUTBUILDINGS AND WORK

----

*T*HE FIRST TIME I WENT DOWN into a root cellar I was apprehensive. It was hard for an outsider like me to tell recently reconstructed cellars from those that were in need of major structural repairs. I had already experienced hazards measuring and photographing other outbuildings; when I tried to measure Frank McGrath's stable, I had to give up since his horses were threatening to kick. Some fishing stages and flakes were precarious to measure, requiring careful balancing in midair on decaying boards; I could only hope that they would bear my weight and not deliver me to the water and rocks below.

But most of the time, recording outbuildings was easy and pleasurable work. The summer day I visited Val Kinsella's premises was typical. He was out repairing the fence to the front yard of his house, but took time to open all the doors to his little group of out-buildings, helped me adjust ladders to the lofts, and even brought furniture and tools outside for me to photograph. I spent most of the day there, and Val got very little of his own work done. Val, like most of my friends in Tilting, never stops working. If they are not fishing or farming, they are making repairs or trying to get ready for the long winter ahead. Tilting's outbuildings are a testament to the diverse and difficult work of the community.

Many individually owned, single-purpose, freestanding outbuild-ings can be found in Tilting today. However, this was not always the case. Dorothy Burke told me that in the past, people had fewer outbuildings, and these were generally larger, multipurpose, and often shared. It is not always possible to understand the purpose of an out-building without talking with its owner, but outbuildings located close to houses include carpentry shops, wood stores, general purpose stores, coal houses, outhouses, grub stores (for storing bulk food), milk houses, hen houses, pig pounds, and garages. (I will discuss those used for fishing and agriculture in the next two chapters.) Though perhaps less an outbuilding than a small second home, I might also include cabins, which appeared at the end of the 1970s. Located in the forest outside

The Kinsella premises outbuildings on the day when Val Kinsella was helping me to take photographs of furniture made by his father, John Kinsella

There was nothing like that up here—you used your own judgment. People knew about the weather, and you'd listen to the older people—you'd listen to your father, if you had one, or your mother too. We often listened to me mother—when she didn't want us to go, well, we wouldn't go when we were younger. When we got older, there were times she told us and we didn't listen to her—but if we did, it turned out she was right—a storm did come. There was weather glasses but you didn't have one. Old John Burke next door had a weather glass—young men like us wouldn't go out and say what's the glass like this morning—he was double our age.

the community, cabins are used for recreational purposes and have taken the place of the old back kitchen of the house as final destinations for old furniture and stoves.

Some outbuildings (like the fishing stage) can be readily identified by their location and appearance, while others may look identical on the exterior but differ in purpose. Both gable roofs and low-pitch ("flat") roofs are used for outbuildings, but builders often select an intermediate pitch. The gable roof was used before the flat roof, and the older residents still prefer it for stages, fish stores, and stables.

It is difficult to determine outbuilding ownership because of Tilting's mixed distribution of houses and outbuildings and its lack of visible land ownership boundaries. While some residents could identify most outbuildings in my photographs, most had difficulty identifying those beyond their own neighborhoods.[1] Although some outbuildings were clustered around their owner's house, others were dispersed within

Left: The Broaders family's outhouse behind their house on Kelly's Island
Right: Margaret Broader's hen house

Mike Greene and some of his outbuildings (left door: milk house, right door: wood shed, right, to rear: snowmobile shed)

DAN GREENE ON THE WEATHER: You went by your own judgment and you watched the wind. You couldn't tell what wind was a bad wind out here on a coast like this. Northwest is bad—but you always knew that a northwest wind and a westerly was the thing to drive you to sea. They were afraid of that more than anything else. A southwest gale and a northwesterly gale, you always had a dread on that when it was coming. You were afraid if it came— if it rose to a gale—it could put you out to sea. The northerly, you had a chance to run—you could go around the Cape, or in Oliver's Cove—or a southeasterly you could run around the Head and go to Joe Batt's Arm or Little Fogo if you wanted to. There was always people living there winter and summer years ago. But that northwest or westerly, inshore fishing or offshore, you dreaded that—that was the thing that put you to sea. That could rise to a blizzard in a minute, and rain, and squalls, and thunder and lightning—in the fall of the year could be snow squalls in it, cold, in September or October. Once you got drove away out to sea out here fifteen or twenty mile off of the Funks you were gone. There was no other shipping, see? There was no longliners—there was nothing.

FERGUS BURKE ON THE FISHING SEASON: I can remember the first of the mackerel—didn't know what it was. Harry Dwyer used to fish mackerel out of Boston. I seen them out here numerous—on the last of the fishing, in August, when you go out in the morning and you see the mackerel, you could say you're finished—all over for this year.

extended-family neighborhoods. Function, circulation paths, land ownership, garden ownership, and harbor access rights determined their locations.

Fred Foley told me the large number of small stores (buildings for storage, rather than retail stores) close to houses is a more recent phenomenon, and that there used to be more gardens around the houses for vegetables. Outbuildings near the house for daily use were placed with great care for efficient access. Dan Greene refined the placement of his outbuildings over the years, moving his combined stable and wood store twice.

Because of their small scale and specialized purpose, outbuildings were launched and changed ownership more than houses. Some outbuildings weighed less than a trap skiff, the type of wooden boat used by a fishing crew to haul cod traps. Jessie and Lawrence McGrath's small general-purpose store behind their house was moved twice. First it was behind the church, then by Justin McGrath's house. Bridget and Greg Reardon's small store moved with their house from Sandy Cove to Tilting. Dorothy Burke's small store across the road from her house on Greene's Point was originally the oil store for the Earle's merchant station on The Rock.

Most of the outbuildings in Tilting are freestanding, but a few are attached, like those at the Kinsella premises. Behind the house is a general store and washhouse. Across the yard to the north are a wood and coal shed, a two-story store (once used for storing twine and now used for carpentry), a stable for sheep, a two-story stable for horses and cows, and a shed for manure. The Kinsella fishing stage is located between these attached outbuildings and the house. The doors to the major outbuildings had a painted ornament, such as a star on the sheep stable and a circle on the store.

In contrast to the more refined paint materials and colors reserved for houses, outbuildings were usually painted with red ochre, and Dan

Top left: Gladys McGrath's general store, just across from the
back door to her house
Top right: Bridget and Greg Reardon's general store, launched to
Tilting from Sandy Cove
Bottom left: Jessie and Lawrence McGrath's general store,
launched twice to its present location
Bottom right: Dorothy Burke's wood store, formerly an oil store
on the merchant's premises on The Rock

DAN GREENE ON FISHING: The old
fellows used to say, "One man is no
good for nothing but two is a crew,"
and so it was. You can't go to the
eastern ground in a boat by yourself.

Left: View of the back of the Kinsella house, with the entrance to the wash house on the right. Across the yard is a group of outbuildings. Right: The Kinsella outbuildings, one of the very few groups of attached outbuildings in Tilting. Sometimes people used compasses to scribe patterns for painted door ornaments. Bridget Reardon told me she painted the round ornament on the door to her store using a dinner plate as a template.

Greene has continued this practice on his premises. The white, painted circular ornament on the door of his carpentry store provides a sparkle in the evening light, almost like a beacon for finding your way home.

Outbuildings were constructed with steep-pitched gable roofs (with either conventional rafters or purlins and wood shingles), low-pitched gable roofs, and single-slope shed roofs. Walls were typically frame construction with partially "flatted" upright (wall stud) surfaces; some interiors and exteriors were sheathed in wood. Some of the older outbuildings in Tilting, like the stable behind Harold Dwyer's house, had full vertical wall studding (no spaces between the uprights) with horizontal clapboard on the exterior and horizontal sheathing on the interior.[2] But the most common construction uses spaced vertical uprights or studs, a light framing method that retains some elasticity through its clapboard and shingle exterior fabric. Houses and outbuildings constructed with this method were easy to maintain, and could be fixed even after suffering structural deformations caused by launching, windstorms, or foundation settlement.

Carpentry shops are one story in height except for Pearce Broader's, which has two stories. There were not many carpentry shops in the

FERGUS BURKE ON SHEEP: There was a saying that you couldn't shear a sheep in May. Shear your sheep in May, and you'll shear your sheep away.

FERGUS BURKE ON GOOD FISHING YEARS: I was in the shop, and there was a fellow that come in there. I don't think I knew the man—that's only recently now—and he said, "Wonderful lot of fish down in Tilting this summer." and I said, "Yes sir. Done well down there, didn't they?" I said, "Sir, I saw more dried up (that's what we used to call [bringing in] the fish, drying up) in one morning at Cronin's Gulch than come over the bar this summer." Boy, you go round Careless Point and there it was—nothing, only boats. From Fogo, Joe Batt's Arm, Seldom, Stag Harbour, Tilting, Cape Cove (Bernard Cluett and them used to come up here)—every one of them full of fish.

past because most people used the first floor of the twine store for this purpose. Fergus Burke told me that unlike the do-it-yourself carpentry situation today, in the past not everyone claimed to have carpentry skills.

General stores were all-purpose stores for household items, tools, and supplies, and they varied greatly in size. Ben and Annie Foley have a "double store." This small, shed-roofed outbuilding is located near the entrance to the back of their house.

Milk houses (creameries) are no longer used in Tilting because today no one keeps dairy cows. Frank Mahoney's family had a seven-by-nine-foot milk house located just behind his house. The roof had a steep-pitch gable roof with the roof sheathing parallel to the roof slope. Margaret Broaders gave me a description of the milk house used by her family when she was young. It was connected to her house by a bridge or exterior deck. The milk house was about ten by thirteen feet in area, and had a gable roof and a door in the gable-end exterior wall. The interior had a plain board floor (scrubbed until it was bleached white), wallpaper made from leftover "breadths" of wallpaper from the house that were applied each spring, and a hatch in the floor that was opened at night to cool the building and covered with linnet to keep the cats out. There was a table covered with oilcloth, shelves covered with white sheeting paper, and a water barrel, and flour, pork, and beef barrels were also kept there.

Alice Greene described the same milk house as it belonged to her grandmother Cecilie "Celie" Broaders. To Margaret's description Alice added that the shelves were along the back wall, the table was toward

Above: Dan Greene in front of his wood store (left) and stable (right). His well-structured wood pile sits to the far left.
Below: Dan Greene's carpentry store, with wood selected for stage and flake repair

Left: Dan Greene's house in summer. His stable is visible to the right behind the house.
Right: Dan Greene's house in winter. The day this photograph was taken, Dan had just come back from a long day on the slide path with his horse.

the front, and there was fly screen over the window, which had two eight-by-ten-inch glass panes. There was a high tea chest between the flour and beef barrel; it had a butter salting tub inside, and you could sit on it. The water barrel was made from a baloney barrel. Alice remembered the look of the bleached pine boards and the smell of the milk in this building. Women had their favorite wooden butter prints, used to decorate butter pats, and Alice had one she cherished with a bell carved on it. In the summer of 1956, an antique dealer came into her house when only her two young children were home. He went into the pantry, took her butter print, and gave the children twenty-five cents each for it. Shortly after, this antique dealer was lost at sea on his way back to St. John's from Labrador with a boatload of antiques.

There were not many separate hen houses in the community because most people kept chickens in the stable to keep them warm in the winter. In the stable chickens were kept in a box made from the staves of a puncheon, but "hen's lice" was a problem for the cattle. If the hen house was separate, sawdust insulation was put in the walls to keep the hens from freezing. Dan Greene had a separate hen house that he banked with snow in winter.[3] Harold Dwyer had a separate hen house in the front garden by his house, with a gable-roof shape and eaves that touched the ground. Val Kinsella remembers that his father would fumigate his hen house each spring by lighting sulfur in a pan that floated in water. After two or three days, he would open the doors.[4] Frank Mahoney told me hen houses were sometimes made from old punts turned upside down.

Above: A ship's cabin found at sea by Harold McGrath, now used as a store by Pat McGrath
Opposite: A star painted on the door of the Kinsella's sheep stable

Pig pounds were either separate buildings or part of the fishing stage. They were commonly located away from the house by the shore. Dan Greene remembers pig-pound roofs covered with birch or fir rind, layered like shingles, and held down with boards. He once had a pig pound just inside his stage door; he cut a hole in the side of the stage and fitted a tierce to this hole to contain the pig in the stage. He sawed off a pork barrel at the quarter point, leaving one stave for lifting, and used it for the pig's trough. He fed the pig with boiled cod's heads, salt fish cullage, and weeds. The pound was outside the stage on the flake and had a bedding of longers allowing easy cleaning.

Outbuildings were sometimes made from things intended for other purposes, such as old row punts used to make cabbage houses. Once, while Harold McGrath was out fishing, he found a small building floating all by itself, partly submerged in the sea. He towed it into the harbor and set it up on land as a small general store. When Harold found this building, it had a slightly curved roof, built-in shelves, and a cabinet. He thought it was originally a ship's cabin from a coastal boat that had sunk.

Houses were turned into outbuildings, most often stables or twine stores, if they were no longer used as dwellings. Allan Keefe moved Fred Saunder's house from Cape Cove to Tilting and used it as a stable.

FERGUS BURKE ON THE "LIGHT IN THE BIGHT"
(SIGN OF BAD WEATHER): Fellows would be beating
in when they had the sailboats before they had any
engines—they'd be beating in the night, the wind would
be off of the land, see? Perhaps moderate all day and
they'd wait until the evening for the wind to rise and they'd
have to beat in, see? And they'd have to tack back from
the light up here in the bight. That was a sign of bad
weather. The other side people used to see it. I saw it
once—only time ever I saw it, it was just like a light. What
I saw—I don't know if we were married or not, after we
got the car, we were over on the other side one night.
We were there by your place, there in the lane. And it was
just like a ship's light—cross the Western Tickle. But they
used to say it was an old schooner, the remains of an old
schooner. I don't know what they are. There are a lot
of them around the Newfoundland coast—can't explain it.

Left: Frank Mahoney's milk house, now used as a general-purpose store, located behind his house close to the shoreline
Right: Roy Dwyer's hen house, previously John and Catherine Kinsella's hen house on The Rock

The purpose of an outbuilding could change: a fish and carpentry store could later be used as a stable. Outbuildings were often constructed from materials salvaged from other buildings. Herman McGrath's stable in Oliver's Cove was built with the beams and sheathing from an old house. Issues of the 1897 newspaper the *Evening Herald* cover the wood sheathing on the walls inside the loft.

While women often visited each other's houses, men visited in outbuildings and often used the buildings as a guest book. For example, on the beams of a fishing stage they would write their name, the date, and perhaps a brief description of the purpose of their visit and the weather conditions. Also, they sometimes listed the names of others present at the time.

FERGUS BURKE DESCRIBES A SEALING INCIDENT: Did you ever hear tell of the time the men were took off of the ice here? That was the 25th of March or so. I was ten—'twas sixty-three or sixty-four years ago. I think it was a Sunday—a fine, fine day. Fellows went off on the ice—way off here I suppose four or five mile—and they got seas. And the next morning, a lot of men went out. The ice parted off. The men that was ashore had to launch punts and they'd go to the edge of the ice and they'd haul them across what they used to call a string of ice. And, you hear tell of Dr. Jones?—well, people used to say they'd never be hear from again if it wasn't for him. He stopped the ice—he stopped the weather or he calmed the seas till the men got off. Dr. Jones had wonderful power—he could cure you. He was a doctor and a priest.

Margaret McGrath's hen house

Tilting's outbuildings provide a wide range of daily sensorial experience. There are contrasts of light and dark, closed and open, dry and humid, quiet and noise. The fishing stage with its open floor of spaced beams, or longers, is open to the air and the sound of the water below, producing a slight feeling of exposure or vulnerability. The stage offers variations in light—the daylight of the open flake or bridge, to the dark stage interior with its small windows, to the brightness of the stage head with light reflecting off the water. The stable is enclosed, dark, soft with hay, and muffled in sound. The root cellar is dark, humid, cool, and silent. You have to feel your way around in the dark. The twine-mending loft and carpentry shop is bright, dry, and warm, and the crackle of softwood burning in the makeshift oil barrel stove provides the background to the sound of conversation and work. In each outbuilding, what you notice first and what predominates in memory is the smell of fish, hay, earth, twine, or wood.

Some of Tilting's outbuildings and workspaces are not specifically men's buildings. Women had to work inside and outside the house, making fish on the flakes, cow hunting, making hay, tending gardens, and even fishing. Tilting women were known for their strength and for their ability to persevere in difficult conditions. As Bonnie J. McCay

Top: Pearce Broader's two-story carpentry store, located behind his house on Kelly's Island
Bottom: Roy Dwyer's milk house, previously owned by Patrick Greene on Greene's Point

ANNIE FOLEY ON MILKING COWS: Them animals knew what they had to do. They'd walk on the path—they'd never go out of the path—walk right over to the fence where they had to be tied on. And you'd put the rope around the horns and that was it.

has written, "Men seek and capture the fish; women process fish and, in some times and places, market fish. In northeastern Newfoundland, women have been critical, though often invisible, in the task of making fish—the labor-intensive and skilled process of converting fresh codfish into a lightly-salted, sun-dried product—the cash crop of Newfoundland's economic history and the source of its value and problems within the world system."[5]

In 1871 James P. Howley made this observation about women's abilities on the water: "I might here state that the women of Notre Dame Bay are just as much at home in a punt as the men and can handle the oars with equal skill. I met many instances of this during the season."[6] Children were also expected to help out when old enough. Describing the shore crew of the inshore fishery, James Candow wrote that it "was often a family affair in which the women and children performed most of the flake work and a good deal of stage work as well."[7]

Still, there was gender-specific work in Tilting. Pearce Dwyer described men's work activities as hunting (for big game like caribou or moose), gunning (for birds), sealing, boat making and boat repair, fishing, house maintenance, carpentry and furniture making, farming, repairing fishing gear, harnessing horses, cutting timber in the woods, slide-path hauling, animal care (except for milking cows and cow hunting), and hauling water (in winter). Pearce listed women's work activities as cooking, cleaning, milking cows and working in the milk house, cow hunting, kitchen garden work, washing and drying clothes, matting, shearing sheep, stoking stoves, sewing, knitting (Pearce noted that some men knitted), washing dishes, wall papering, making fish, making hay, and hauling water (in summer). However, in the past women did not work for pay. Many jobs, such as cutting up firewood, caring for children, making fish, making hay, picking berries, and planting, trenching, weeding, and harvesting gardens, were shared by

DAN GREENE ON GUNNING: In February northern slob would come and the water would calm. There was no water for ducks to pitch, so they pitched in the gulches. They'd pile right in—they'd pile up—they'd get that thick in February, frosty night. They'd be on top of one another, they used to say. The fellows with the muzzle loaders, they'd creep down and you couldn't light your pipe—if you lit your pipe, they'd smell the smoke and leave it—they were cute enough for that. The men would have white suits on, white cap—they'd give them two guns, a 3/4 or a 7/8—with a handful of powder and wad it and then put in your shot. They'd kill perhaps a hundred then—they'd hook them ashore there. You had a line, a reel, like a fishing reel, and a floating jigger—a jigger for hooking birds. A piece of wood with hooks nailed all around it. Every man had one of them on his back. It could take a while to hook them—sometimes a gunning punt was used but you had to be careful not to blow offshore.

FERGUS BURKE ON MODERN FISHING: They don't work at all now. They got their gurdy—put their door line on the gurdy, start their engine, and when they got their fish dried up, shove out their net and put their rope around the gurdy and hoist it up, and it'll all drop down in the bottom of the boat.

FERGUS BURKE ON TRIPS INTO THE BAY: After the first of October, they used to break up the boats—take up the pounds separating the fish and get ready for going in the bay. They'd make a couple or three trips in the bay and get their wood for the winter, anyone that didn't have a horse. There was people who never went in the bay, I suppose. Anyway, there would be two or three brothers, and they'd have a fair-size boat—no power in them—nothing, only the sails, see? Say I was living alongside of someone who owned a boat, well, I'd get a chance to go in the bay with him and they'd give me a share of wood. You'd wait till you could get a time in the bay, then. They'd beat out the harbor, wind in from the northeast—tack back and forth—then they'd square away, round the Head or the Cape, whichever way you liked. Now that was a little before my time. I can remember the boats though.

The workbench in Allan Keefe's stable

men and women. In winter men took care of animals, but women helped
with the animals in summer.

Dorothy Burke's husband, Louis, took care of the cows, horses,
and sheep, and she took care of the hens. Dorothy spent a lot of time
cow hunting. In early summer cows would go among the alder trees to
get away from the flies. Women would hunt them down in the forest and
milk them. It could take a long time to find them, but you could not
leave cows longer than two or three days without milking. Women were
responsible for milking the cows and making butter.

Men's relaxation and social areas were sometimes more public
than women's social areas, extending to outbuildings, retail stores,
wharves, lookouts (viewing gallery rocks), and merchant's premises.
Until about twenty years ago, only men used remote cabins in the
woods for camping trips; both men and women use these cabins today.

One thing I don't understand about the inshore fishery right now—it's failing. But my people used to always have schooners. And there was years, around the early 1900s, they used to have to leave here to go to Labrador to get fish—there was no fish here, not a fish. Well, there was no draggers, no nothing out here, only there was the sailing vessels, the dory men, the Portuguese, they were out here, the Frenchmen, the Spaniards, that's all, no beam trawlers—I was on the Grand Banks meself when there wasn't a trawler there from the other side—and at the same time, there was bad summers here, no fish at all. So, it wasn't 'cause the fish was getting caught then (by draggers) that caused that, well—what caused that in them years? Our people made two trips to the Labrador (in a thirty-five ton small schooner: larger than a bully boat). The first time they carried cod traps and they got a load of fish—they come home, took it out, and the next time they left home the traps and went down hand lining—and that time they was four men of 'em, and they got eighty quintals, that was twenty quintals a man (salted fish) and they got back here in October. Well, that was late—they made the two trips—no fish here that summer. The draggers wasn't catching it then. Must have been the temperature of the water or something, or the capelin.

CHAPTER 6

FISHERY OUTBUILDINGS

*I*T IS NO SURPRISE THAT the most prominent outbuildings in Tilting were its fishing structures. Fishing stages, twine stores, fish stores, and flakes were important parts of everyone's property, and still surround the harbor today.[1] After the construction of the community stage in 1965 and the founding of the fishermen's cooperative on Fogo Island in 1967, Tilting's smaller fishing stages were not used to their full potential. Fish is now brought to the large community stage on The Rock for shipping to the cooperative for processing. But many fishers still use smaller stages for tying up their boats and for storing equipment. For a short time in the fall, they may process some salt fish for family consumption.

Pearce Dwyer told me each year the fishing season started after the predictable yearly storms of Peter and Paul on or about June 29. Cod traps were not set until after this date and were taken up around July 20. But in recent years, before the closure of the cod fishery in 1992, few cod traps were used. Gil netting for cod started in mid-June and lasted until mid-September. Trawling for cod started the first of July and lasted until mid-September. Hand lining for cod started in mid-August and went until the last of September. Families fished for their own winter fish supply in the fall of the year, from mid-October until the last of October, using hand lines and short trawls.

Dorothy Burke told me that in the fall, the men went out fishing in the morning. When they came back, they washed the coarse salt off

Top: The inside of Mike Greene's fishing stage
Bottom: Elevation of Mike Greene's stage, showing the placement of foundation cribs known as "ballast beds" or "ballast lockers"

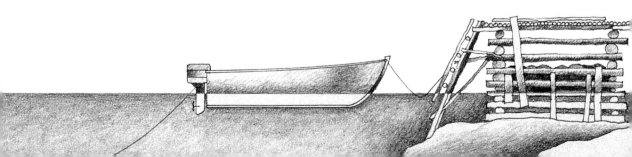

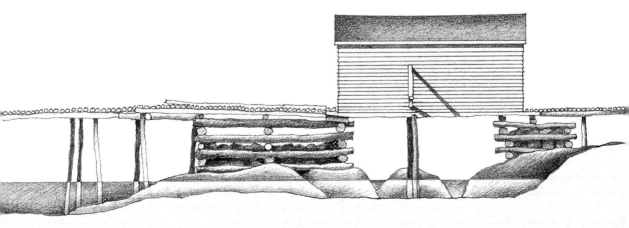

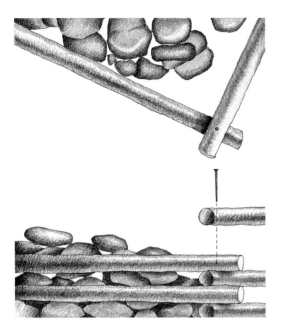

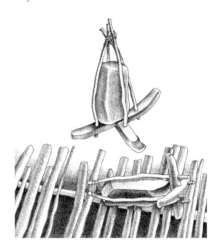

previously salted fish, then the women spread this wet fish called "waterhorse" fish on the flakes in the afternoon (often the children helped). Women worked together to carry barrels of fish and spread it on the flakes or on rocks to dry, taking care not to expose it to the full sun (sunburned fish was lower grade). They would place it face up one day and face down the next, and bring it in every day at around 5:00 P.M. Spreading fish often took two or three hours, and drying it took five days in good weather.

Herring nets were used from mid-October until late November, and from the beginning of April until about May 10, if there was no ice. Lobster pots were set between May 20 and July 15, but in Tilting there was no lobster fishery until the early 1950s. Capelin would come into shore to spawn around June 20, and casting nets were used to catch capelin; capelin season lasted only a week or two. Small bait fish called lance were caught off Sandy Cove beach. You could not count on the squid fishery every year, but, when they were available, jigging for squid (also used for bait) lasted from the end of August to the end of October.

Markers for cod trap fishing berths were dropped on June 1 at 12:00 A.M. each year, and men who wanted a berth had to station themselves in advance on their desired mark. Fergus Burke told me if there was ever a dispute about trap berth locations (when berth markers were dropped at the same time and place), then lots were drawn for the berth. When Fergus was young, trap berths were set close to shore. Later they were set offshore, sometimes as far as a mile. Net mesh had to be larger than four inches in those days. The more men you had to haul the trap the better, as the old cotton cod traps were heavy. A cod trap that Fergus and others made had a ten-inch mesh in the doors and needed at least three men to haul. If too much fish was hauled in the trap for the size of the boat, then a cod bag was used.[2] These were nets separate from the cod trap, used to keep the fish alive until they could be brought in later, after the first boatload of fish was delivered to the stage, or shared with other fishing crews in the vicinity who were experiencing a poor catch (men used to lace the bag on the head of the trap). Pearce Dwyer told me some of Tilting's fishers used what were called "share traps." These were owned and repaired by Earle's, who received a share of the catch in exchange for the use of the trap.

FERGUS BURKE ON MARKING COD TRAP BERTHS: I used to hear me father telling me about it—they were in Oliver's Cove in the night—him and uncle 'Lonze. And twelve o'clock they used to drop the poles—and some of the fellows were getting drowsy I suppose, and he was a keener. And anyway, his two brothers were with him— they were going for a berth. Anyway, when he saw the chance, he twigged the other fellow—the other fellows had their punts moored down in Hurley's Cove, you see? They jumped aboard their boat, and when they hauled her off, the grapelin was down and they couldn't get the berth. But now, you can go up to the hall and draw your berth.

Almost every family fishing crew had their own regular cod trap berths. Pearce Broaders's was in the center of Wild Cove. When fish would come in there, they would also come into Oliver's Cove. Fergus Burke recalls, "When you'd hear tell of the fish in Joe Batt's Arm, just as soon have it as if it was in the stage. Because they'd come down around Round Head and go in Wild Cove." Charlie Brett from Joe Batt's Arm fished at Wild Cove Rock. Billy, Mike, and Austin McGrath's berth was outside of Bob's Gulch. Mike Greene's father, Pat, was also at Bob's Gulch; Pat Reardon took over his berth (he also used Wild Cove Point and the Western Point of Pigeon Island). Gilbert Dwyer and Philip and William Broders were at Pad Keefe's Point. Fergus Burke's father, William, used the Green Gulch Rock and also fished at Oliver's Cove and at Careless Point. Mark Mahoney fished at Sweeney's Rocks. There was a trap berth at Black Rock, but never much fish there. The Carrolls had a cod trap at the eastern point of Pigeon Island. Lambert Greene had a berth at The Rock of the Head. Pat Greene was at Long Point (men from Joe Batt's Arm also fished there), Cyril Dwyer was at Nance's Point, and Herb Sexton fished

View toward The Rock and the community stage, constructed by the government of Canada in 1965 (photo courtesy Bonnie J. McCay)

Ben Foley's capelin drying on a frame in front of his double store

at Higgin's Gulch. Tuck's Sunker was a berth used by a trap crew from Noggin Cove (near Carmanville across the bay).

Fishers from other communities came to Tilting to fish, but each year the fish would arrive in the bay before they arrived in Tilting. Seldom-Come-By men moved from the bay to Tilting to follow the fish, as did Stag Harbour and Noggin Cove men. Some fishers even came to the Tilting area in schooners and motorboats from Fogo, Bonavista Bay (St. Brendon's), and Wesleyville. Island Harbour men also fished near Tilting. Fergus Burke told me that William ("Billy") Butt from Island Harbour, the father of many sons, was heard to say, "There's only seven of us down this summer—the other four's on the Labrador." Dorothy Burke described the fishing scene in Tilting when she was young: "In the past, fish were plentiful in Tilting. You would not get through with them boats anchored in the harbor. People would come from other communities and anchor their boats in the harbor, from Joe Batt's Arm, Change Islands—split their fish on board. This practice stopped thirty years ago."

Albert Cluett's fishing stage on The Rock. His carpentry store is behind the stage to the left, and visible in the background to the right is his brother Ned Cluett's house, floated to Tilting from Cape Cove.

Usually fishers from Tilting did not range beyond Round Head to the north and west, but they sometimes fished at Cape. Fergus heard a rumor from years before his time: "The Greenes [John Greene and Martin's father, Lambert Greene]—they rowed three hundred quintals from the back of the Cape—in a row skiff. Three hundred quintals in the season." (One quintal is 112 pounds.) Most Tilting fishers did not venture past the Breaking Rocks.

From wherever they caught their fish, Tilting men brought it home to their fishing stages. James Candow aptly describes fishing stages as amphibious structures "which served as a bridge between land and sea." He notes their obscure ancestry and their architectural form, character- izing them as enclosed wharves, or hybrids of wharves and ships, similar in structure to the "North American Iroquoian longhouse and the Beothuk smoking or drying house for fish and game."[3]

Dan Greene's fishing stage is one of the finest in Tilting. I take a walk with Dan from his house down to his stage, presently used by his son Art.[4] We head down the narrow lane, surrounded by an old-style

Clockwise from top left: John Kinsella's fishing stage on The Rock, with a view of the Cluetts' houses and outbuildings in the background; Kevin Greene's fishing stage on the southwest side of The Pond; Fergus Broder's fishing stage near The Gulch; Gerard Greene's fishing stage on Greene's Point

picket fence that was once common throughout the community. We pass by his carpentry shop, once used as a fish store for drying cod. This building used to have a top floor, called a "loft" or "twine loft," with a small iron stove in the northeast corner like the ones used on fishing boats. The loft, with its coped ceiling and four-foot-high sidewalls, was used for mending cotton nets.

We head out to the stage on a long, elevated wooden flake or bridge, walking on the centerboard planks for comfort. Dan tells me these planks could be used to separate fish from two men who were drying on the same flake. You need a wide flake to dry fish, and Dan's flake used to be wider. We reach the stage doors with their painted white ornaments (Dan used to have horseshoes on the doors for good luck). The doors have carefully fitted, hand-carved wooden buttons to hold them open in the wind, and also built-in wooden handles. Dan explains that the stage head on the harbor side of the stage required wide doors called "window leaves"; they practically opened up the entire end wall. They were designed to ensure that the wind did not catch them when they were open. Dan's window leaves slide into a wooden slot, but another type hinges up to the ceiling.

Some stages had just one door at the stage head, but with wide doors you could bring your punt into the stage for storage during the winter. Dan's father had bully boats, which were pulled up on the land for storage, but Dan only used punts and could store two in the stage. The wall framing of Dan Greene's stage is similar to the framing of his row punt. Art keeps his fiberglass motorboat bottom-up on the land. These days punts are no longer put in the stage in case a storm damages the stage. Dan lost his fishing stage, his punt, his hay, and items in his store in a big storm in 1935.

Dan pauses in his description of the fishing stage to tell me what it was like "on the water" while fishing on the Eastern Ground. He always worked up a good appetite on the fishing ground, and he would have a meal from his breadbox of bread, butter, and tea. He would catch fresh cod and fry it in fatback pork using the small iron stove in the cuddy of his boat. If he had another fellow with him and Dan was aft catching fish, the other fellow made the fire. Sometimes they would have a meal of jowls (fish faces) and hard tack bread. Then they boiled the kettle and made tea from loose tealeaves.

Dan Greene's stage silhouetted in the fog. The outline of the fish splitting table is visible inside the stage.

A view to Dan Greene's fishing premises, showing what the old lanes looked like before roads were widened and paved for cars

Dan Greene's fishing stage with the stage head bedding and strouters in place for the summer season. From left to right are Arthur Greene, my mother Hetti Mellin, and Dan Greene.

Fishers used a hook and line when their boats were anchored on the shoal. Dan said some fellows had three lines going at one time: two on one side and one on the other. Dan said hand lining was "terrible hard on your hands, there was never anything like it." He remembers the early days when bait was placed on large hooks that had no eyes; these were later replaced with swivel hooks with eyes. When the tide would run, he would put two leads on the line or the line would be carried away. The line had to go down ten to thirty fathoms to get to the codfish. Dan used squid jigged in Sandy Cove Bight or Wild Cove for bait ("They didn't come in other places"). The codfish ate best in the evening or at night, and a storm or breeze made the fish active. Some days there were no fish, and Dan feels the tide was the culprit.

We step inside the stage, and Dan comments that his present splitting table would have been larger in the past. There is a semicircular

JIM GREENE ON BULLY BOATS AND FISH POUNDS: When the schooners died out, the bully boats came in, about seventy years ago the first bully boats came in here—same thing as a small schooner, only he had the engine in her. Martin or John got the model of the bully we built.... A pound would hold twenty-five quintals of fish. That was a square box. You'd have what they used to call pound boards—keep the fish stationary—keep it solid. When the nape of the fish is right level here and the salt is in it, the salt can't fall away from the fish and it's holding the pickle more. You'd put twenty quintals of fish in that pound, and you'd go along and you'd make another pound, another twenty quintals of fish in it. Well, the trap men, they'd have the whole length of the stage—they used to bring in fifteen to thirty barrels each trip—they didn't keep twine or nets in the stage. The trawl man wouldn't want a splitting table as big as a trap man. We used to have chutes—the sound bones and the cod's heads go out in the water—if that would hang up on the land the flies would cause maggots.

Dan Greene's row punt

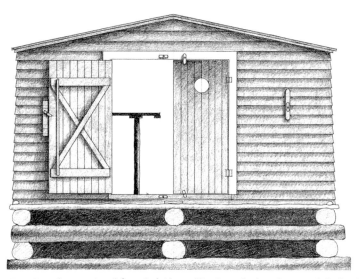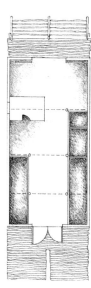

Dan Greene's stage viewed from the bridge and in plan. The doors have carefully fitted wood buttons to hold them open in the wind, and also built-in wooden handles. The plan shows the position of the splitting table and fish pounds; the stage head and "window leaves" are at the top.

cut in the edge of the table for splitting fish, and a small wooden cleat is nailed to the top to help hold the fish. If there were two splitters, there would be another cutout and cleat in the table. After splitting, puncheons were used to hold the fish; these were later replaced by tierces with wooden runners underneath. Dan made his own wooden box with runners to hold the fish.

Dan explained that preparing the cod involves five operations: tending table, cutting the throat, heading, splitting, and salting after washing the fish off in a puncheon. If only two people are working in the stage, one person cuts the fish's throat and head and picks out the liver (for cod liver oil) and the other splits the fish. If there is a four-person crew, there are two splitters, one header (who has to work very fast), and one person to tend table (take the fish from the floor or bedding of the stage and put it on the table). Large crews worked in stages that were much longer than Dan's present stage. Today about the only Tilting stage long enough for this is Ambrose McGrath's stage.

Dan's son Art now uses the stage just for storing fishing gear and for salting a small quantity of fish for the winter. A cow's carcass fresh from slaughter hangs inside the stage from the rafters, where it is cool and well ventilated. The meat will later be cut up and frozen. Also, pigs

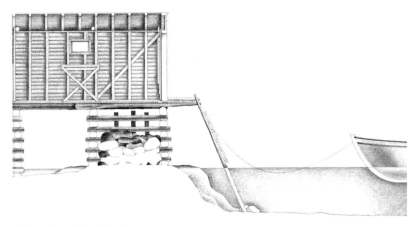

Section through Dan Greene's stage

are often slaughtered in fishing stages. The stage floor or bedding is made from "flatted" longers, timbers shaped with an axe, with one- or two-inch-wide gaps between them to let water and debris pass through. A plank floor would require too much work to keep clean. A draw bucket is used to wash down the stage, and a trunk hole in the bedding is used to draw up water. Ideally, the trunk hole should be located by the splitting table. Fish offal is thrown down through a heading hole, away from where clean water is drawn. Next to the splitting table is a small hole in the wall leading to a chute for discarding the sound bone (the back bone of the cod fish).

Dan tells me there were mostly gable-roof stages in the past to help keep the stage from leaking in the rain. His stage has a support placed on top of the collar tie to hold the ridge beam of the roof. His present stage is the third or fourth stage built in this location. The current stage is around twenty-five years old, and some of its bedding was saved from the previous stage built by his father. His father's stage was about forty to fifty feet long, and the stage before that one was sixty to seventy feet long. Large stages need to be braced to resist

ROSE BURKE ON HAND LINING: That's another different fishing altogether. They go out—way out on the grounds and they're out all day and they jig. They don't have trawls or traps or anything like that. That's when they get their winter fish.

JIM GREENE ON BUILDING STAGES: You get what they calls ranging beams, great big long beams on each side, the sills of your stage—you only wants two of them—you're going to have your stage twenty, thirty feet long, whatever it is. Put your ranging beams on top of your wall—the breadth you wants it—then you put on your bedding. You got to flat your ranging beams—you got your side flat, and you got your top flat, the other two sides, no odds about them. The side flat got to be straight—you got to put your uprights set down on that—got to be clapboarded, whatever you're going to do with it.

You can flat the bedding sticks if you want to on one side. If your stage is wide, maybe you wants another ranging beam between those two, or maybe two. I built one down there not a hell of a while ago—I sawed the wall sticks off square and stuck them down on the ranging beams—but the old fellows had great big, terrible big stages and they used to mortise them down and everything. For the roof you puts on your couples, same as anything else—as a store or anything else you'll be building. They used to put in stringers—they had to be stringers in between the couples. The roof would be steep—not covered. But when they built those flat-roof stages they covered them with felt. Well, they thought it was going to be more easier to build—that's the reason—and so it was easier to build but it was no good to keep fish! Felt on a hot day in the summer is real hot—and brings in flies—and flies brings maggots—see? It's no good—it's good, but it's not as good as the old-fashioned gable-roof stage with no felt on no nothing.

Fishing stages on Little Fogo Islands. Although similar in construction to the fishing stages in Tilting, these are oriented with the long dimension parallel to the shoreline.

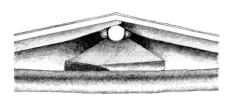

Above: A section through Dan Greene's stage at the collar tie for the roof structure, and a drawing of a carved wooden salt shovel
Opposite: The spar shore on Mike Greene's stage. This beam is installed over the exterior ranging beam with its thin end wedged under the central ranging beam. A force applied to the spar shore can easily be resisted with this arrangement.

wind forces. Dan calls these braces "push braces"; Jim Greene called them "spar shores." These ingenious braces, which are on Mike Greene's stage, not only resist wind loads, they also help the exterior walls to resist the heavy weight of the salt fish bulks. The braces are constructed by lodging the top of a long tree trunk under the center beam of the stage. Its butt end projects through the stage bedding and cantilevers over the side ranging beam of the stage. The cantilever is about four or five feet long, with a notch cut into the top to anchor the bottom of a diagonal brace for the exterior wall.

Fishing stages are always one-story buildings. Fergus Burke remembers both gable- and flat-roof stages were in use when he was young. Purlined roof construction was used for the older type of gable-roof stages, as it provided extra protection from roof leaks. If there was a leak in the wood shingles, the sloped orientation of the sheathing that resulted from this construction directed water to the eaves. Most

JIM GREENE ON THE LARGE STAGES OF THE PAST: The Greene's had one over there, one that got carried away in that tidal wave—it was thirty-three feet wide and had three wharves under it. It was a big stage and could hold about four hundred quintals of salted fish. And there was lots of more stages just as big as that. A lot of people had small stages—fellows that was fishing hand lining, he didn't need it big—but take five or six men with two or three traps, give them four or five hundred quintals of fish, they wanted a big stage.

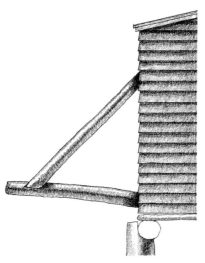

JIM GREENE ON SPAR SHORES: Clapboard right on your uprights is good enough because if you're goin' saltin' fish in that stage you got to board her up inside—so far up—just as high as you'd salt fish. The beams that stand outside the walls of the stage, you know what they're for? When you salt a big pile of fish in the stage, maybe five feet high, you salts it fresh. Now then, after a week or so that fish she's going down all the time—when that's going down, that fish, it's also forcing out, and after a while it will force the side right out of your stage.

stages were the longer type, about sixteen feet wide and thirty-five feet long. Stages used by trap crews were longer than those of fishermen who worked alone. The smaller stages were called "singlemen's" or "one-handedmen's" stages. At that time stages also extended further out over the water. After some stages were lost in storms, most were later relocated closer to land. Still, Tilting has some unusually long bridges to access its fishing stages because of the need to reach deep water in the center of the harbor. Some of these stages cross paths in midair, reflecting the complexities of property ownership along the shoreline. Fishing stages on nearby Little Fogo Islands are similar in construction to the fishing stages in Tilting, but many are short stages with a parallel orientation to the shoreline. This is probably a result of Little Fogo's steep coastal terrain.[5]

If the stage was located over the water, the fish could be unloaded onto a wooden platform directly outside the stage head. If it was located over land, a less desirable location, then the fish had to be unloaded to a remote wooden platform over water and carried to the stage. These platforms were sometimes removed in winter to prevent ice or heavy waves from damaging them.

Stages were painted with the same color scheme as other outbuildings: red ochre for clapboards and yellow ochre for trim. A gable-roof stage was considered by some to be better than a flat-roof stage

JIM GREENE ON SPAR SHORES: Those things that stands out there with those spar shores coming up against it, they're put there to keep the side of the stage where it won't go out. I'll tell you a story now about them things. There was two men over there—one man's ground comes next to the other's. Well, this old fellow, he built his stage right over to his boundary. And then, he put in those spar shores and they're out over the water that goes into the other man's stage—and that old fellow wanted him to saw off them spar shores because it was sticking out over his water. I'd stick his head down on the bottom if it was me! No, he didn't saw them off, no! Spar shores can be made from a big longer that goes right across your stage on top of the range beam level with the rest of your flooring and stands out about four feet outside of your stage. And out on the top of your beam, you put a notch down there—and you cut away your shore so it will fit that slope. You understand it? And then you nail on your clapboard, and you stick that thing down there to get the length up where it is at an angle and you take a maul and you drive it down solid and it can't get out of there 'cause it's notched down—stick two or three nails up here and there you got it—and fish can't force the side out of your stage no more. All the stages had them.

Interior of Basil Lane's fishing stage

Clockwise from right: Basil Lane's fishing stage near The Gulch; Lawrence Lane's stage (now demolished), showing the use of a large rock for a corner foundation support; Gerard Greene's stage (left) and Dan Greene's stage (right), with their bridges crossing in midair

because it has better ventilation for curing salt fish in the summer. The door to the stage in the gable end was off center, reflecting the layout of the fish pounds (bins) for curing the fish inside. In the stage Fergus's father used, immediately inside the door (the "upper end" of the stage) there were fish pounds on both sides of a three- or four-foot-wide aisle. On one side was a three-foot-wide pound, called the "long bulk," extending about fifteen feet along the exterior wall. On the other there were pounds of fish arranged in three-by-ten-foot "short bulks" perpendicular to the aisle.[6]

Fish were "pronged" from the boat into the stage (Fergus told me they used to say, "stick it in the heads"), and a stage headboard across the threshold was used to retain the unloaded fish. A dredge barrow was used to haul fish around the stage. According to Fergus Burke, children used to rock in it to play. Small windows in the stage were located at the splitting table, at the stage head, and sometimes at the "upper end," but never where the fish curing in the pounds would be exposed to the sun.

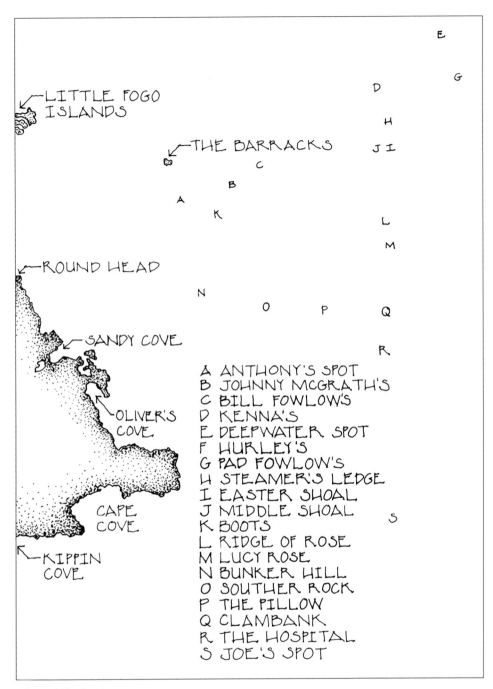

LITTLE FOGO
ISLANDS

THE BARRACKS

ROUND HEAD

SANDY COVE

OLIVER'S
COVE

CAPE
COVE

KIPPIN
COVE

E

G

D

H

J I

C

B

A

K

L

M

N

O

P

Q

R

S

A ANTHONY'S SPOT
B JOHNNY MCGRATH'S
C BILL FOWLOW'S
D KENNA'S
E DEEPWATER SPOT
F HURLEY'S
G PAD FOWLOW'S
H STEAMER'S LEDGE
I EASTER SHOAL
J MIDDLE SHOAL
K BOOTS
L RIDGE OF ROSE
M LUCY ROSE
N BUNKER HILL
O SOUTHER ROCK
P THE PILLOW
Q CLAMBANK
R THE HOSPITAL
S JOE'S SPOT

Above: Fishing location map
Opposite: Allan Keefe's stage, located on an island close to shore. Only minimal foundation work
was required to provide level support for this stage.

174   TILTING

JIM GREENE ON MAKING FISH PILES: You don't know how to make a pile of fish—I'm able to make a pile of fish where the rain won't go through nowhere—and when I get me pile of fish made where it go up small to one fish—when I had it made to height I'd turn over me frame and put it down on top of it. You'd have to alternate it. You put the first ones down face up, then you put the other ones back up on top of it. Now, when the two tails come together here, you go across with another tier of fish in the middle, and as you goes up you narrows your pile of fish. Some people take a pride about how good they was with making a pile of fish—oh my god, yes!—and some women could make them—my god—fancy! That's right: you'd know who made that pile of fish—I walk down over the bridge, I'd know what woman made that pile of fish—no water'd go in there. There was half-quintal faggots and two-quintal faggots, three-quintal faggots, you made up your faggots you could tell how much fish you got—how many pounds. Four-quintal faggots were also made on the flake, but any more than that you make it in round piles.

Allan Keefe's stage, built by Allan, James, and Dave Keefe in 1943, is probably the most frequently photographed fishing stage in this part of Newfoundland. It is situated on a large, smooth rock offshore, but requires minimal wood shoring for support. Allan's wooden boat would just fit inside the stage, and originally the stage had a boat slip. It used to stand on a small island further offshore, so in order to avoid punting fish from the stage to the shore, it was relocated around 1975. It has deformed over time, resulting in a sloping west exterior wall. The last time this stage was used for processing large quantities of salt fish was in the 1960s. The stage was too damp to "finish off" the curing of salt fish, so it was finished off in the twine store. This stage was recently restored by the Tilting Recreation and Cultural Society (TRACS).

Twine stores were usually two-story buildings located near the shore by the stage, with either gable or flat roofs (twine stores built recently are usually one-story buildings).[7] These buildings had a wide exterior door to accommodate wheel and hand barrows, accessed from a ramp where possible but never from a stair. Good light was required for preparing fishing gear in the store, so windows were usually placed on more than one of their second-floor exterior walls. In winter the first floor was used for carpentry, general storage, and as a grub store for bulk foods like flour, pork, and beef. In summer this floor was used to store linnet or fish. The twine store was an all-purpose store and could also be used for wood storage. The second floor, or shanty loft, was used for mending linnet and storing twine in winter, had no ceiling, and was heated with a small wood stove ("If you got a lot of twine, you wants a big store."[8]); it was not used in summer unless sharemen were staying there. Often a hatch was placed in the middle of the second floor for pit-sawing lumber.

Clockwise from top: Gerard McGrath's twine store on a small island by the McGrath fishing premises; John Kinsella's twine store (with steep pitch gable roof); Pearce Broader's twine store on Kelly's island, one of the larger twine stores in Tilting with central beams and columns supporting the floors; Harold McGrath's twine store, painted in the traditional colors of red and yellow ochre; Herb Sexton's twine store, the top floor of which was used as a "shanty loft" for sharemen's accommodations in the summer

Gerald Reardon's twine store was owned by the Bryans, who owned it until 1924, then by Joseph (Jos) Dwyer. After that Clarence Foley kept sheep in it. One of the sheathing boards is twenty-two and a half inches wide, remarkable considering the small dimension of timber available in Newfoundland today. The beams of this twine store were sometimes used as a register for men's visits: "Clar Foley, October 27, 1924. Cyril Foley, Norris Arm, September 6, 1948. November 5, 1993: Mike Keefe, Ray McGrath, Gerald Reardon. Killed the last of my sheep."

Mike Greene's twine store also has writing on the beams. This building was originally a house, built around 1880 by Clarence Greene. Patrick Greene removed the interior partitions and turned it into a store. The back kitchen was removed, and the building was launched to its present site. Fred Greene used to make coffins here.

Harold McGrath's father, Michael McGrath, built his twine store around 1937 with the assistance of his sons. The lumber for this store was shipped in from Carmanville across the bay. The first floor of this two-story twine store with a low-pitched gable roof was used in the winter for storing traps, nets, and other fishing gear, but in fishing season was used for the final curing of salt fish.

Fergus Burke told me his family's twine store was fourteen by sixteen feet, and some twine stores were larger. Today there are not many large twine stores. Kevin Greene's is one of the last large ones in Tilting. Large twine stores were used by trapmen. When Fergus was young, many families had trap crews: Greene (two crews), Burke (two), Sexton (one), Carroll (one), Bryan (one), Davis (one), Tobin (one), Mahoney (one), Broders (one), Dwyer (one), Foley (one), McGrath (one, but two or three before), and Reardon (one).

Albert Foley had a separate, vertically studded fish store. He told me they used to let the fish "work" in this store before shipping it to the merchant. Will McGrath also had a separate fish store with a low-pitched roof. Fergus Burke told me there were not many separate fish stores in the past. He described the merchant's use of a culling board for grading dry codfish. Up to twelve inches was tomcod grade, twelve to eighteen

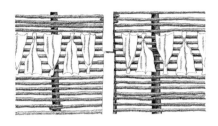

Flake bedding and foundation details. The wood bedding and salt fish layers alternate thin and thick ends.

The flake and bridge to the stage and twine store of Albert Dwyer's premises. A walkway has been constructed on top of the open bedding of the flake for an easy and safe access path.

JIM GREENE ON FLAKES: The whole other side over there was covered with flakes. You get on a flake down there at Greene's stage and walk right to Coleman's Lane without getting off a flake—one fellow's flake right tight to the other. The flakes were always on the harbor side, always next to the stage. You come right out of your stage, you're out on the flake. We used to have to lug fish from down here, cover over all those hills with fish—spread it out over the rocks—that's after two days spreading it out on the flake. You couldn't put fish that you just washed out on the rocks 'cause on warmer days the sun would burn it up.

inches was medium grade, and eighteen inches and over was large grade. Beyond this standard the culler used his own judgment to decide if the grade should be extra large.

Fish flakes are elevated wooden structures used for drying fish. Sometimes they had a dual purpose, as a platform for drying salt fish and as a bridge for fishing stage access. They once provided a nearly continuous raised network of circulation between fishery outbuildings in Tilting. Many stages in the community extend a considerable distance from land to give access to deeper water, and a single-purpose bridge would not have been efficient. The working platform consisted of longers covered by spruce or fir boughs, and the boughs could be removed at the end of the fishing season. The wood bedding and the salt fish layers alternated their thin and thick ends. The bedding was supported by large beams,

The McGrath flake, one of the last flakes used for drying salt cod in Tilting. In this picture, taken in 1987, Ray McGrath is standing on the flake.

which were supported by wooden shores similar to those used for house and outbuilding foundations. The palette of raw materials and details used for flakes was also used in picket fences and woven "riddle" fences. Planks were placed in the center of the longers for walking on or for wheelbarrows. Nearly all the flakes disappeared in Tilting a few years ago, but some have been recently restored by TRACS.

Jim Greene told me that when the weather was unsuitable for drying fish, it was placed in small piles on the flake and covered with a tentlike, clapboarded structure. This structure was completely enclosed, but ventilated through the bedding of the flake. By the time I arrived in Tilting, several of these wooden fish covers were being used on the ground near houses as hen houses.

We'd go in the fall of the year—we'd pick out a spot of woods—say twenty, or thirty, or fifteen loads of wood, whatever the case may be—we'd cut a trail up through that wood—and when the snow would come, we got a shelter for our horse. The horse is in the lun—he's not out in the open, and the grass [the horse's hay] blowing away from him—or perishing to death—he's in the lun, same as we are. But we wouldn't cut that wood around that horse—we'd go so far—and spell it up to the slide! You see? And on the tail end of it we'd cut it—finish up that spot of wood. We'd shift to another place, put our horse in—but now, you'd only go a hundred feet. That's far enough to spell wood—that's a good load, then. But now, they come in and they clean it all down—pick out the prime wood, and they'll only bring what they call a butt joint. They cut off that about eight or nine feet. The rest of it is left in the woods to rot. You see? Before, your horse would go in and they'd take the whole length of a tree. But today, they take the butt joint. The best of the wood is left in the woods to rot. Now they [snowmobiles, ATVs] can go everywhere, you see? Wherever there's an open they can go.

CHAPTER 7

AGRICULTURAL OUTBUILDINGS, FENCES, AND GARDENS

----

*I*N MY FIRST YEAR IN TILTING, just before sunset on a clear, warm day in late August, I took a walk from my house down to Greene's Point. Terry and Anthony Burke were raking hay in their meadow, collecting it in large linnets. We dragged the hay to Terry's small stable nearby, where it would become winter food for Bob, Terry's Newfoundland pony. The intensive hay cutting and harvesting in the community made me aware of the unique agriculture outbuildings in Tilting.

Outbuildings for farming—stables, hay houses, root cellars, and cabbage houses—are usually located some distance away from the house in Tilting, sometimes even in or adjacent to remote outfield gardens. Stables and hay houses were designed to provide dry, well-ventilated conditions, but root cellars and cabbage houses had the opposite character. They were subterranean structures, designed to keep vegetables moist and cool but also to protect them from frost.

Stables were used to keep horses, cows, sheep, and chickens.[1] Occasionally, the final cure of salt fish was done in the stable in summer. They could be either one or two stories high with either low-pitched or steep-pitched gable roofs. Stables were sometimes combined with other buildings, like twine stores. Fergus Burke recalled one two-story double stable that was used by two families. Typically, the first floor of the stable was used for animal pounds and the hen's nest, and the second floor as a hayloft.

On some premises the stable was located fairly close to the house to make access easier in poor weather, but stables were not attached to houses because of their smell. When Ted Burke lived in Cape Cove, he used to tie a rope from the house to the stable to find his way back and forth during a blizzard. People were afraid of going astray, of falling over the ballicaders (large, thick, sloping sheets of ice along the shore) and drowning. Snow banks made by the snowplow would pile up against Dan Greene's stable door. This would delay slide hauling, so he moved his stable from the other side of the road to the back of his

Terry and Anthony Burke pooking hay on Greene's Point

Ambrose McGrath's stable on Bunker Hill, formerly located in the McGrath neighborhood

Lawrence McGrath's stable, now cut down to a one-story building. A manure pound is attached to the barn to the left, and to the right is an addition for extra hay.

Herman McGrath's stable in Oliver's Cove, now owned by Desmond Greene

Gerard McGrath's stable in McGrath's Cove

Frank Foley's stable in Sandy Cove, formerly Ambrose Reardon's stable

Lawrence Broder's stable at Lane's Rocks

Martin Greene's stable across the road from his house

Basil Lane's stable, with wood stacked to dry against the gable-end wall

house. The stable that Fergus Burke's family owned was large, about sixteen by twenty feet, with six feet of clearance to the underside of the beams on the first floor.

    Jim Greene thinks an ideal stable for a horse, cows, and sheep is eighteen by twenty-two feet. A six-foot ceiling height is required for a small horse, and an eight-foot height for a large one (thirteen hundred weight). He prefers the gable roof to the flat roof, and the roof pitch should be "all according to what you thinks is right yourself." With a large horse and a four-foot second-floor wall height to the bottom of the gable roof, the height on the corner post would be twelve feet. When I first saw the Lane house in 1987, Mike Lane had a small one-story

JIM GREENE ON ANIMAL HUSBANDRY: There was one winter I had three horses here meself—the boys was hardy enough to work the horses and we got the horses and they went away in the fall to work and I was home all the winter with three horses. I had cows, too—cows and bulls and sheep and—there was years we had three cows. We used to have five and six sheep—we used to have chickens, piles of chickens, I don't know how many—ten, fifteen chickens. We used to have a chicken house out behind the barn, that's gone now—it was separated from the barn. You wouldn't have chickens in the barn—'twas too dirty and 'twould make the animals dirty too—hen's lice. Also, the hens don't want it that warm, and in the barn where there'd be a lot of animals that barn would never freeze out there—it was too warm for the sheep.

stable for his Newfoundland pony. The stable was located across the lane from his house near the shoreline and next to his wood store. This building was just barely large enough for the pony to fit (ten by ten feet with a side-wall height of six feet), but she seemed not to mind (the gable roof provided more headroom toward the center). At the time there were several stables like Mike's on other family's premises in Tilting, but most are now gone. As of the summer of 2001, there were only three Newfoundland ponies left in the community, and only a few families now keep sheep, goats, and chickens. Raising cattle or pigs for meat is rare these days.

Hay houses or hay sheds were remote buildings that were always located in hay meadows. In winter a trip to the hay house was required every two or three weeks with three or four linnets. People hauled hay to the stable in a linnet holding eighty to one hundred pounds of hay. In the past these linnets were specially knitted from twine and had a "running string" and a five- or six-inch mesh. Sometimes part of an old

JIM GREENE ON SHEEP: Now, at one time, we wanted sheep because—all my family—the women knitted all their gloves, all their socks, their sweaters, their underwear, and everything. Now they are better off. They don't have to shear the sheep, wash the wool, spun it, card it, knit it—that's a lot of work—the women used to do that to keep their family warm. You don't have to do that no more, so, they can do away with the sheep. They're not going to have no mutton to eat—we always had plenty of mutton to eat. There was bags and bags of wool, and since my wife died we give it away. So, what are you going to do with the animals? That fellow's fishing—if he can do away with his and live without 'em, I got to do the same thing—I got to do away with me horse if I can't get fish enough to get money enough to get a skidoo and haul me wood that way. Well, you can go to the relieving fellow. But there's somebody else keeping you going—you're not doing it yourself. And, to me, that fellow is no good! If he can't even get wood to keep his family warm, get fish enough to get them something to eat, and keep sheep, and all that—if they makes him do away with his horse and do away with his sheep, it's going to be harder on him—'tis a bigger burden.

Cyril McGrath with his sheep on Little Fogo Islands. In the spring of the year, he takes his sheep over to these islands in his open motorboat, and he brings them back to Tilting in the fall.

Sheep shearing at Mike Lane's premises

Desmond Greene's hay house in Oliver's Cove, with minimal foundation supports

cod trap was used for a hay linnet. Some people used a square linnet with a rope attached to each corner; others used a punt sail. Most of the present-day plastic linnets are from fishing nets.

Fergus Burke recalls five hay houses at one time in Tilting—two at Oliver's Cove, one at The Farm, one at The Meadow near The Pinch behind The Gulch, and one not far from Higgin's Height. Hay sheds were discontinued because they were inconvenient in winter (hay kept in stable lofts was much more accessible), and only a few remain in Tilting. I recorded two of these, one at Oliver's Cove, owned by Desmond Greene, and the other on Roy Dwyer's premises. There was writing inside Roy Dwyer's hay house: "VK [Val Kinsella] June 15, Friday 1956 fencing. Kenny Broders, August 9, 1951."

The hay houses that Fergus remembers were always one story with an area of ten by twelve feet or twelve by fourteen feet, a flat roof, and no windows. They had no wood sheathing inside or out, just clapboards nailed onto the outside of the uprights. Longers were used for diagonal bracing on the inside of the hay house. These braces provided an air space between the hay and the clapboards to help dry the hay. All the interior wood surfaces of Desmond Greene's hay house have been polished smooth over several generations from friction with the hay.

Hay is hard won in Tilting. The growing season is short, and there is only one cutting per year. Hay is gathered from every garden, and nothing goes to waste. Mowing starts around the third week of July, but some people wait until September to mow. Hay is easier to cut in wet weather because the dampness keeps the scythe sharp. Usually, the hay is left to dry where it is cut. In the evening it is formed into

Desmond Greene's hay house, with its wood polished by years of hay storage. The longers bracing the walls help the hay to breathe along the exterior wall, which is made without sheathing under the clapboards to ensure good ventilation.

JIM GREENE ON REGULATIONS AGAINST OPEN GRAZING: All over Newfoundland, they got to be barred up, haven't they? Well, if they got to bar up their animals here, they got to do away with the animals—they can't keep them. They got nowhere to bar them up. If they want to keep the animal in the winter, they haven't got that much land to bar up the animals—they'll have to let them go, and then you're in trouble—they can't do it. There was one time, maybe those people that's running the council—maybe they can live without the animals—but the average poor fisherman, he can't live without his animal. He wants a horse in the winter to go pull firewood to keep his family warm unless he's well enough off to get a skidoo and haul his wood that way. If he doesn't have enough land to feed the horse in the summer, he'll have nothing to feed him in the winter and he'll have to do away with him. And 'tis going to put a hardship on him, but if there's enough rich people or people thinks they're rich—well off—to be able to live without animals on Fogo Island, that's it—the other fellows got to suffer. The poor fellow's got to suffer.

Left: Albert Cluett cutting hay with a hand scythe in the front garden of Harold Dwyer's house
Below: Pooks of hay in Sandy Cove. Hay was put in piles called pooks to keep it dry in case of rain.

"pooks" with homemade wooden rakes, two hundred pounds to a pook. These cone-shaped mounds protect the hay from rain. If it rains overnight, you have to wait until the ground is dry to spread the hay for drying. Hay spread on the ground has to be "shaken up" two or three times a day. Once dry, the hay is hauled to the stable in a linnet. If the distance is short, you carry the linnet on your back. In the old days, the hay was hauled by a horse and hay cart (Frank Mahoney called it a "horse and wheels").

Albert Cluett taught me a lesson about hay cutting. He lives down the road from our house, out on the end of The Rock. He still has Tilley ("Til"), a senior registered Newfoundland pony who has foaled almost every summer these past few years. Albert needed hay for Tilley, so, having noticed the grass in our fenced-in front yard was long and going to waste, he stopped by to ask permission to cut it for hay. He worked on it all day with his long-handled scythe, cutting with the regular, practiced rhythm of over fifty years experience, a pleasure to

Top: Jim, Cyril, and Andrew McGrath cutting hay in Sandy Cove
Bottom: Mike Greene turning hay near his brother's house on Greene's Point

DAN GREENE ON CUTTING HAY: That style, that way of life is gone out. They don't cut it like that now. The land, they don't till the land, they don't grow hay like that now. They don't mow it—you hardly see anyone mowing hay. Them times, every garden you see a man or two in it, all his clothes threw off, and down right to the bare pelt sometimes—pants, belt around his waist, although he might have on some kind of slight shorts—he'd cut this field of hay and dry it and stack it in pooks. If you couldn't get it home—I seen times when you couldn't get it out of Oliver's Cove—you put about a ton of hay in two pooks. Ten hundred pounds in each pook. It wouldn't blow out of it—wouldn't blow away.

watch. He then carefully raked the hay into pooks. The next day, after making heavy bundles of hay with linnets, we put the hay in the back of my truck and brought it to his yard near his house. I thanked Albert for transforming our wild front yard into a neat lawn, but he was not finished yet. He returned to our yard, took out his pocketknife, and for the next hour he trimmed the grass around the boulders and steps. He appreciated access to the hay, and I appreciated help with the yard. But for me this was not a simple transaction, and the memory of that day stays with me. I was humbled by his demonstration of care for the land.

Hay houses are not the only agricultural outbuildings disappearing from Tilting. Before 1930 there were two types of cellars for storing root crops, both made with a wood frame and covered with sod. One was accessed through a hatch on the top and the other on the side (the side-hatch cellar is no longer popular because of problems with the accumulation of snow around its entrance).

Alice Greene explained the process of constructing a root cellar. An area was dug out, and then the hole was framed with saltwater logs (there was a seasonal harvest of these logs, often drifting pit props—"They drive into the coves"). The logs were placed tight together vertically, and barrel staves were nailed horizontally on the inside of them. Either pork barrel staves or molasses puncheon staves would be used. No barrel staves were nailed under the roof logs, which were placed in gable-roof fashion on the sidewalls. The roof in Alice's cellar was covered with felt, followed by three or four layers of sod.

Dan Greene's root cellar behind his house on Greene's Point. The large cross-sectional drawing shows the construction of Dan's cellar. The small drawing on the left shows the traditional roof construction of a root cellar, with birch bark used in layers like shingles to shed water.

The roof in Dan Greene's root cellar is lined with layers of birch bark like shingles to shed water. Protective banks outside the cellar were built up with layers of sod after sawdust was packed around the structure for insulation.

Vegetable pounds were framed between the walls with boards. Small potatoes were placed in the outer pound and were used first; seed potatoes were left in the inside pound. March was the worst month for penetration of frost, so some people kept a lantern going in the cellar at that time of the year. Cellars are often fenced in with picket fences to prevent animals from digging in the sod and climbing onto the roof, and to help to retain the sods placed around the outside of the cellar. After 1930 concrete cellars were occasionally built, and these were identical in form to the old wood-frame cellars except that they used a piece of railway iron to support the roof and did not require

Dan Greene's root cellar on Greene's Point, not yet mowed   *Dan Greene's root cellar after mowing*

birch rind for the roof. Fergus Burke's family had an eight-by-ten-foot concrete cellar, built in 1932 when he was eight years old.

Herb and Alice Greene had a root cellar with a side-access hatch at Sandy Cove Hill. Herb built two or three root cellars in his lifetime, and this one was built in 1963. The cellar had a porch (vestibule) formed by inside and outside hatches. They would stuff the porch with a bag of grass for insulation. The outside hatch was slanted and covered with felt, and it had a handle on it. This was a large cellar with pounds to the side on the interior for easy access. There were three pounds: one for turnips and two for potatoes. Gerard and Margaret McGrath later owned this cellar.

The root cellar was too warm for cabbage, so separate cabbage houses were constructed. These were usually made from old punts that were turned upside down, placed over a hole or well-drained depression in the ground, and covered with one or two layers of sods. Boards or sawn-off pickets were nailed to the gunnels of the boat to retain the earth around the sides of the hole in the ground. The door to the cabbage house, about three or four feet high, was placed in the stern of the boat. Cabbages were stored with the roots on, and sometimes they were hung by the roots from the punt. Temporary cabbage houses could be constructed by digging a hole, covering it with a "cooling tub" (made from part of a puncheon), and banking it with snow. The cabbage stored in this temporary structure was not used until the spring. Fergus Burke's family built a cabbage house without using a punt. It was six or seven feet wide and twelve feet long. It had a strongback beam (a ridge beam), but not much sod on top.

Above: The damp, cool, and dark interior of Desmond Greene's root cellar
Left: The exterior of Desmond Greene's root cellar in Oliver's Cove. You would never know this is a root cellar unless you saw the hatch at the top of the small grassy mound.

JIM GREENE ON THE CELLAR INTERIOR: You put a partition down the center, and a partition across the upper end—only have a square pole right underneath the hatch. You can reach all the pounds. Seed potatoes were kept in a special pound to themselves. I used to heave them all in together. I'd have two hatches, one right down low, right where the roof begins, then you have the other one on top—and then I'd fill a couple of oat sacks full of hay, and I'd put them between the two hatches, and every time I'd go to the cellar I'd lift them out.

First thing, you got to get a good place to build it. That's a hard thing to do. That's the worst job you got, trying to find a good place to build that cellar. On a hill is the best—you don't have no water. You get down a hollow, you're sure to have water. We built this cellar so it would hold about twenty barrels of potatoes and two or three barrels of turnips—maybe seven feet by nine, something like that, and about five feet high. You log it up inside—the best way to have the logs is vertical because whatever moisture is in that wood drains away from it—if it's horizontal, it lodges there and rots quicker. You just lay them on the ground, and you have stringers, back and forth, maybe on the inside or you can have them on the outside—you put your wall plate on top of that, then you

Allan Keefe in front of his root cellar in Oliver's Cove

put your strongback, and board her over on top. Now they use logs for the roof, but at that time they used to use puncheons—you knows puncheons, the staves? The right length for to make both sides— that's plenty strong—inch oak—and there's not a hell of a lot of weight on it—the strongback has all the weight. You wants about two feet of sod on top—after it's there for a year, you don't need two feet, but for a new cellar, you wants two feet. I always had the entrance through the top. Some people has it in the ends—but then, you gets a big patch of snow, every time you go to the cellar you have to carry a shovel—but mostly always there's no snow on top of the hatch.

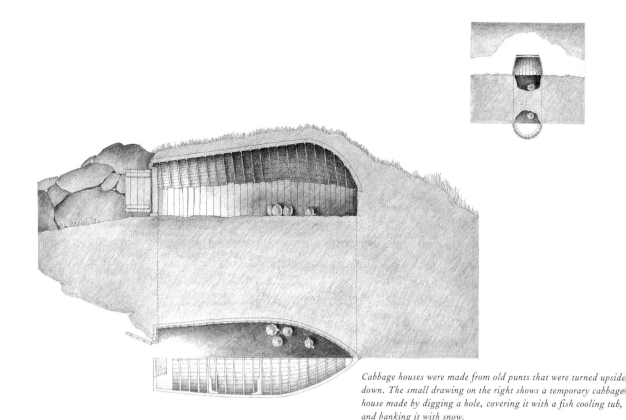

Cabbage houses were made from old punts that were turned upside down. The small drawing on the right shows a temporary cabbage house made by digging a hole, covering it with a fish cooling tub, and banking it with snow.

JIM GREENE ON CABBAGE HOUSE CONSTRUCTION:
We had a different place for the cabbage—we had a cabbage house. There's a hollow up there in the cliff, you'll see it—that's where we had our cabbage house—a big notch running alongside of the cliff. We had an old punt—carried it up and turned it bottom up on top of this gulch—and we boarded up the holes around between the gunnel and the bottom and covered it over with sods and put a hatch in the side of it and O.K. A cellar's too warm for cabbage—it doesn't need so much earth on it or anything. Leave the roots on the cabbage and stick the roots right on the ground—press them right up tight to one another. If you had some cabbage left—not room enough for it in the cabbage house—you ties four or five cabbage heads together by the stumps and hang them up on nails from the roof of the cabbage house. They keep that way, too—good.

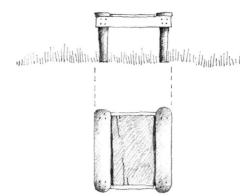

A hand barrow   *Dan Greene's portable carpentry bench*

In Tilting agricultural items often borrow their forms from fishing implements. As cabbage cellars are formed from row punts, rakes, hoes, and scythe handles are made from the same raw materials used to construct fishing stage beddings. Their wooden pickets and longers are processed in the same way, hand-stripped of their bark by rinding with an axe. This is done not only to make the material more resistant to decay but also to make it comfortable to handle. If the bark is left on the pickets and longers, moisture becomes trapped between it and the wood, and this accelerates decay. Also, this is unsightly, as the bark from spruce and fir bark tends to fall off over the years in ragged strips. Longers are also used to make kelp barrows, hand barrows, waterhorse fish barrows, box barrows, three-stag (or prong) barrows (used by four persons to carry twine), barrel barrows, and wheel barrows.

Another convenient carrying device is the water hoop, used for hauling water. These hoops were made from split saplings lashed together, and sometimes from old apple barrel hoops. A person would stand in the hoop and balance the handles of two water buckets on it, making it much more comfortable to carry water long distances. A similar hoop with a smaller diameter called a "wits" or "withe" was used to latch a gate.

The most visible use of wood is in fences. Because of open graz-ing of animals, fences in Tilting were used to keep animals out of gardens, not to pen them in. Paling fences, longer fences, and picket fences are still constructed in Tilting. Longer and picket fences were

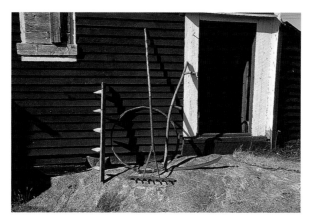

Agricultural tools and a traditional water hoop on the Kinsella premises

rinded to make them last longer. Paling fences were more refined and were always painted; they were reserved for use around the small front gardens of houses. The top of some of Tilting's palings were cut in the shape of a steep gable roof with narrow shoulders at the bottom of the gable. The paling fence and gate on Dan Greene's premises is painted white with green accents. The gate is carefully constructed and operates with a counterweight suspended from a pulley on top of a pole.

Clarence Foley described another type of traditional fence; it is no longer used in Tilting. This fence had pickets driven into the ground and a horizontal cleat nailed to the top of the pickets on either side. The cleat was split first, with the flat side placed against the pickets. In another variation on this fence, a longer was placed over the top of the pickets. A continuous notch was sawn out of this top plate to accept the pickets. Thus no nails were required for this type of fence. Clarence remembered a fence in Sandy Cove that had this detail.

Another type of fence once found in Tilting was the riddle fence, known elsewhere in Newfoundland as a "shortlar" fence. This fence

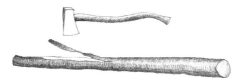

Far left: Locally made wooden hoes and rakes
Left: Stripping bark with an axe, locally called "rinding." Wood tends to last longer with the bark removed, and the appearance is neater.
Opposite: Allan Keefe with a locally made wooden rake, photographed outside his stable

A "wits" or "withe" made from saplings, used to latch the gate in the fence behind the Kinsella house on The Rock. These hoops were also used to hold the oars in rowlocks in punts.

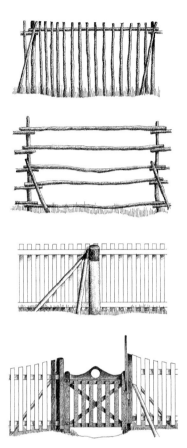

Top to bottom: Traditional fences found in Tilting today: a picket fence, a longer fence, and a paling fence; Dan Greene's front gate, operated with a counterweight and ornamented to match the doors of his outbuildings

was constructed by weaving very long and thin pickets between three horizontally placed longers, alternating the weave for each picket; few nails were required. The pickets were left long to project high in the air, and they were woven closely together. This made it impossible for anything large to get through. The riddle fence's name suggests the form of a sieve; only small animals and the wind could get through it.

Strong fences have been critical for Tilting's gardens. Herb and Alice Greene had a typical complement of gardens for their family's needs. They had two vegetable gardens by Sandy Lookout, a hay pasture by Pearce Dwyer's house, three hay pastures in Oliver's Cove, and a

A fence constructed in the summer of 2001 around the garden containing the Sexton's twine store

JIM GREENE ON DESTROYING THE ENVIRONMENT: Them skidoos are destroying the trees—they run over the small trees, tearing them up. That same fellow—if he had to fence a garden, drain it, put seed in it, and grow hay and feed a horse—that fellow would never be in the woods doing that. They are destroying the forest in on Fogo Island. Now, if you got some way of getting handy to them politicians, and tell them what is happening in the outports and in a place like Fogo Island—what they are doing with those skidoos—they chase the caribou in here on Fogo Island. The fellow on the horse can't—he can't do that because he can't go over that bank of snow cause he's only going to have a path where he goes in every day. The skidoo driver goes all over the place, takes the tops off the young trees. I wouldn't stay here, I don't think—if I was a young man, I wouldn't stay here.

Hinge in the front gate to John and Alice Green's front yard

vegetable garden near the road to Oliver's Cove. The walk from their house to Oliver's Cove took about fifteen or twenty minutes.

A generation or two ago, kelp for garden fertilizer was stockpiled on the beach from October through December, moved back from the high-tide water line. Each family made its own pile in Oliver's Cove or Sandy Cove. A kelp barrow was used for this purpose, with linnet between the staves of the barrow. The kelp would rot over the winter, and the salt would leach out making it suitable for fertilizer. Kelp was hauled from the beach to the gardens in March using a horse and slide. The kelp was dumped in piles in the gardens. March and April was a time for fence repair also. Leftover pickets from the store of winter wood were gathered for this purpose. In May and June the kelp was spread on the gardens, and in June the soil was turned.

DAN GREENE ON FENCES: Sheep are nice. I love sheep and horses. No trouble to keep them out if you have a half decent fence.

JIM GREENE ON RIDDLE FENCES: We had a riddle fence—it had no nails. The last one was here was over back of Terry's. The picket fence and the longer fence you could run out and go over, but this bloody riddle fence, you couldn't climb over that. You could keep in anything or keep out anything. Riddle fences were made from boughs and longers—you could use spruce, fir— they had three longers—alternate weaving—there was nowhere to put your foot to go up, and there was spears sticking out on top—you couldn't go over that so you had to keep away from it.

June was the start of planting season. Today potato planting is still done in the traditional way with beds and furrows. Planting occurs before the third week of June, before the capelin come in. A week or so before planting, seed potatoes are cut from the supply in the root cellar. These are allowed to sprout a bit, spread on the floor of the store or spread outside if there are no chickens ranging about the premises. After the soil is turned, straight lines are struck for one-foot-wide furrows. The ground is subdivided into two-and-a-half-foot-wide beds, and the beds are coated with kelp. Seed potatoes are placed on the bed ten inches apart. Earth from the furrow is shoveled onto the seed to a four-inch depth. After three weeks more fertilizing is done with capelin or fish offal, and this is covered with soil. This process is called trenching. After this two weedings are required, but no watering has to be done.

It takes about ninety days for the potatoes to be ready for harvest, but an earlier meal of potatoes is possible some years. The potato stalks are dug out with a handmade wooden hoe. You stand on the potato bed and work forward, putting the potatoes behind you. These are covered with potato stalks and left to dry on the beds. Later they are brought to the store where they are spread on the floor to dry for forty-eight hours. In the first week of October, the potatoes are placed in the root cellar. Large potatoes for seed are put in a separate pound.

JIM GREENE ON SECURITY: They're making more money than ever I made fishing here, but they haven't got the same security that I had, and I can't explain why. My people had no money, but they had plenty to eat—they had sheep, they had cows, they had vegetables, all kinds of potatoes, plenty of salmon, plenty of herring, plenty of fish, plenty of ducks, seals in the spring, you couldn't starve then, but they had no money—and they had plenty of clothes to keep them warm, and they had all kinds of wool— plenty of wood. In the big city, people were starving.

ANNIE FOLEY ON "LUGGING UP KELP":
Holy week was the week you'd bring the kelp—because you'd be in the church for Holy Week and the smell of the kelp off people's feet—and you wouldn't have second pairs of boots to change. Be in the kelp all day and you could smell it off our clothes. Good rotten seaweed.

Top left: Longer fences (left) and picket fences (right) near Bunker Hill
Top right: A garden in Oliver's Cove with traditional cabbage and potato beds
Bottom right: A riddle fence, a type of woven fence that provided a very effective barrier to keep animals out of gardens

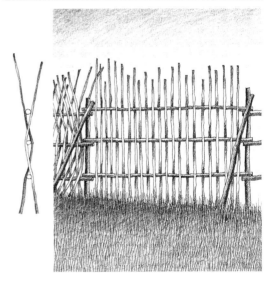

Cabbage is grown from store-bought seed and is planted after the third week of June. It is planted in a slightly wider bed than the bed used for potatoes.[2] Three cabbage heads can be grown side by side in a three-foot-wide bed. Furrows one foot wide are placed between the cabbage beds. Kelp is placed on the beds before seeding, and seed is placed eighteen inches apart and covered with one-quarter inch of soil. Three weeks later the plants are up. They are then trenched with capelin, but no earth is used to cover the capelin. On a small plot of ground, the leftover seed is sown, and plants from this plot are transplanted as needed. Only one cabbage weeding is required, and the cabbage is ready for harvest in sixty days.[3]

Me father was going to Halifax or going to Maine. And there was a song called "Dear Newfoundland Have I Got to Leave You." And when the steamer backed off from the wharf, he was stood up on the bridge and he started to sing it. The captain stopped the boat and waited until he finished singing it. He was some singer—he'd lie down on the couch and sing all night and the next day and never sing the one song over and over again. And there was an old Irishman there on the boat—and he begged my father to go to Ireland with him—he said, "It won't cost you a cent." And I never hardly believed him.

CHAPTER 8

REBUILDING AND PRESERVING

----

*I*T IS HARD TO BELIEVE that the unique small-scale structures once so common in Newfoundland and so strongly associated
with our vision of its architecture and landscape have disappeared faster
than the codfish. Tilting is one of the last places in Newfoundland where
you can still see the full range of vernacular structures associated
with the family-based inshore fishery. Of all the communities on Fogo
Island, Tilting has preserved the most intact traditional cultural landscape; its settlement patterns, animal husbandry, agriculture, traditional
houses, outbuildings, and artifacts like furniture and tools are unmatched
in this region of Newfoundland.

Isolation may partially explain the persistence of things like
old houses and fishing stages in Tilting, but a better explanation may
be found in the island culture of the people. Tenacity and courage were
required to survive in this remote, harsh environment, and a scarcity
of supplies and general hardship inspired people to make do with local
materials and construction techniques. Tilting's residents had to be
able to make many of the items they needed. Boats, houses, and furniture
were locally crafted well into the 1950s and 60s; these were often based
on traditional designs and often used recycled materials. New forms
came slowly; house types like bungalows and split-levels were adopted
almost twenty years after they became popular elsewhere in
Newfoundland.

In recent years the community of Tilting has begun to realize
the value of its heritage. Though there was initially resistance to
preservation efforts, there is now an enthusiastic local heritage movement. Several historic houses and fishing premises have been restored
by the Tilting Recreation and Cultural Society (TRACS)—a volunteer
association that relies on local labor for its restoration projects. TRACS
receives donations of buildings threatened with demolition. It then
restores the building on the owner's premises if possible, or launches
it to another site. Two restored houses in Tilting—the Lane house and
the Dwyer house—were the recipients of Southcott awards from the
Newfoundland Historic Trust. A third Southcott award was recently

A restored row punt on Albert Dwyer's premises

presented to TRACS for the partial reconstruction and restoration of the fishing stage, flake, and twine store on Albert Dwyer's fishing premises.[1]

TRACS's goal is to preserve and restore all of the remaining vernacular houses and outbuildings in Tilting, and also to preserve landscape features like fences and gardens. They are also committed to conserving things like locally made wooden boats, furniture, and traditional crafts, such as hooked mats. TRACS has also completed part of an extensive network of walking trails in and around Tilting. The organization is to be commended for using authentic construction techniques and materials in these projects.

The Lane house (a project started by TEA—the Tilting Expatriates Association—in 1994) provides a good example of the quality of restoration work being done in Tilting. This the oldest house in Tilting, and it is now used as a local museum. The cooper Augustine MacNamara (known as "Augie Mac") built the house sometime prior to 1836. After MacNamara drowned at Black Rock Tickle while on a trip to get kelp from Sandy Cove Beach, Aeneas Dwyer purchased the house. Dwyer sold it to Dick Cashin, who sold it, through Donovan Burke, to Laurence Lane. Laurence Lane's son, Mike Lane, was living in the house when I measured it and provided much helpful information on the history of the house.

In the late nineteenth century the Lane house was transformed by a new second floor addition that combined two types: a center hall house superimposed on an existing hall and parlor house. Clarence Foley told me the story he heard from his father about this renovation. Aeneas Dwyer owned the house at that time, and his daughters complained about the low ceilings on the second floor. "He started in the morning and finished at night. They didn't have to shift out of it." Versions of this story I heard from others also emphasized the skill of the builder in completing the exterior of the renovation in only one day: "never a drop of water got in." (The second floor cooped ceilings are still low by today's standards.)

These photographs show Albert Dwyer's fishing premises, recently restored by TRACS. The top photo shows (left to right) the house, store, stage, and twine store. The photos below show the twine store, previously owned by Kyran Burke and his sons Cyril, Tom, and Louis. Inside are slides for hauling wood by horse.

With Dwyer's changes there was a conceptual separation between the two different house-plan types, but the facade trim boards help to resolve the tension between the two. The problem of reconciling the pattern of three windows (second-floor center-hall plan) over two (first-floor hall-and-parlor plan) is solved by the first-floor center trim board, which substitutes as a third architectural element. To achieve a special effect, clapboards were placed on the diagonal to fill some of the small panels between these trim boards.

The remnants of the rafters of the earlier house are still visible in the gable-end walls of the attic. They seem to form a king post–type detail, but it is not certain if king posts were present between the gable-end walls. The profile and dimensions of the original house, based on the outline generated by the original rafters, were similar to Tilting's Davis house. The second-floor bedrooms have cooped ceilings, and the second-floor window sashes slide vertically for ventilation.

The original interior wood sheathing on the Lane house was carefully done. I suggested leaving out a section of wallpaper so that the sheathing boards could be exposed in the living room. These boards were pit-sawn and carefully hand-planed, then fitted with tongue and groove edges. They were tapered along their lengths (following the profile of the tree trunk) to efficiently utilize the raw material. Tapered boards had to be installed in alternating courses in order to keep things level.

The house's semicircular staircase is the only one of its kind in Tilting. It is not certain if this was part of the original house or if Dwyer added it. It has the character of form, fit, and finish that suggests that the maker could very likely have been the original owner of the house, the cooper Augie Mac. Fitting stair partition boards and stair treads and risers in a circular pattern would have been easy for a cooper who was used to dealing with compound curvatures in his daily work. The builder could have simplified construction by compromising either the handrail or the attic stair, but he chose instead to demonstrate his skill and carefully wove the two together.

View of the Lane house from Kelly's Island

The semicircular stair in the Lane house was possibly constructed by the original owner of the house, the cooper Augustine MacNamara. A section had to be structurally rebuilt and reinforced as part of the restoration work.

The plan of the Lane house stair is shown on the left, with the attic stair outline shown with dashed lines. On the right is a drawing of a corner kitchen dresser that was made by William McGrath, painted white with red trim.

TED BURKE: We used to give away a lot of stuff, you see—now them times, boy, 'twas hard times—way back in the thirties. Well, like the fellow said, "When you're down, 'tis hard to rise." Well, there's Mart, and Fred, and Sam—they had a big family. So, lots and lots of nights, boy, or in the evening, we'd go out, or our mother, go out and get this bucket—heave them out a piece of beef in it, heave a peace of pork in it (we used to always bring the barrel of beef, we'd never buy any loose stuff, we'd buy our barrel of beef, our barrel of pork,—barrels of flour at that time, four or five barrels of flour, and peas and beans and prunes—and all our winter's diet), and a bucket of potaties, 'cause we had plenty of land and we used to always have plenty to eat and we used to have the onions grew. And carry it up to Mart this Saturday, and carry it up to Sam next Saturday, and carry it up to Fred next Saturday. Oh yes, we really helped our neighbors. Well, that's what we're supposed to do. We're put in this world to help our neighbor—and if we can't help our neighbor, 'tis not much odds about it. Now that's the way we looked at it, you see?

Restored fishing stage on Reardon's Island, summer 2001. The roof sheathing boards are placed on purlins or "stringers."

The nearly completed reconstruction of a fishing stage on Reardon's Island with the construction crew in the summer of 2001. From left to right, they are Ern Keefe, Cyril Broders, Herb Burke, Jerome Dwyer, Walter Bryan, Gerald Reardon (foreman), and Peter Penton. Missing are Aidan Adams (from Joe Batt's Arm) and Tim Penton.

projects were overcome when I learned that outbuildings were traditionally reconstructed and launched. The original locations of some of the wharves could be determined by their underwater foundations, and the sites of many stages and flakes have been verified by consulting archival aerial photographs. One of the main things lacking from these restoration projects is the clutter of original tools and equipment that you can still find in many of the family-owned fishing premises in Tilting. However, many artifacts that would otherwise have been discarded or lost have been donated for the restored premises.

Every few years in Newfoundland, tourism and economic development proposals surface to recreate a traditional fishing village for tourists somewhere in the province, often in locations where no fishing stages, flakes, twine stores, people, houses, outbuildings, or gardens remain. Substantial government funds are allocated for proposals and consultants, while authentic, living, working communities like Tilting are ignored. Apart from modest but much-appreciated regional employment support, Tilting has received very little government funding. With all the preservation and tourism work that has been done in Newfoundland in the past two decades, it is curious that there is so little emphasis on the authenticity of the buildings and on preserving a complete community or household.

Even though there are presently no heritage preservation regulations in Tilting, several families have always maintained their premises in their original condition. For example, the Kinsella premises, established in 1918 by John and Catherine Kinsella, contain one of the most remarkable collections of material culture in the province. Located on The Rock at the tip of the peninsula in the most prominent part of the harbor, the site includes a house with its multiple additions, a unique grouping of attached outbuildings, a fishing stage, and an extensive collection of furniture and artifacts made by the owners. No public funding was used to preserve and maintain these structures. The authenticity and sense of history of the Kinsella premises will never be challenged by fictional re-creations of outport life—they remain a wonderful testament to Tilting's heritage.

The persistence of aspects of Tilting's traditional way of life and the survival of its traditional buildings in these modern times is an enigma. While global culture creeps closer to Fogo Island every year, people in Tilting continue to farm, keep animals, visit their neighbors, live in family neighborhoods, and fish. It is also remarkable that today's community is willing to preserve not only its old buildings but also the techniques needed for their constant renewal. I hope this book will call attention to the importance of this fragile architecture, and that people will remember how a small group of settlers banded together to survive in an isolated, inhospitable landscape, far from Ireland, and made it their home. As Annie Foley once told me, "We done all right."

A view of the Kinsella premises from the Cluett premises, showing the fishing stage, attached outbuildings, the house, and the general store and washhouse

NOTES

Introduction

1. Until the mid-twentieth century most of Newfoundland's rural population was dispersed in small coastal settlements called "outports," and many of these were accessible only by sea.

2. Bonnie J. McCay, "Fish is Scarce: Fisheries Modernization on Fogo Island, Newfoundland," in Raoul Anderson, ed., *North Atlantic Maritime Cultures* (The Hague: Mouton, 1979), 155–188.

3. James P. Howley, notes from 11 November 1882, in William J. Kirwin, G. M. Story, and Patrick A. O'Flaherty, eds., *Reminiscences of James P. Howley: Selected Years* (Toronto: Champlain Society, 1997), 193.

4. Indian Islands are a chain of islands just off the south coast of Fogo Island; Little Fogo Islands are shown on the map on page 174.

5. In the 1950s and 1960s, the provincial government attempted to resettle residents living in remote communities to new or existing settlements. Joe Eaton was the last person to live in Cape Cove. Cape Cove had a school, and the teacher was usually from Tilting. The school was also used as a church. Elizabeth Cluett, interview with the author, Brigus, 1987.

6. Ted Burke, interview with the author, Tilting, 1987. Many similar interviews provided me with substantial information throughout this book. These interviews were conducted in Tilting and St. John's between 1987 and 2002. Although I am indebted to all of the interviewees, for brevity's sake each quote and reference will not receive a note herein.

7. Bonnie J. McCay, "Appropriate Technology and Coastal Fishermen of Newfoundland," Ph.D. dissertation, Columbia University, 1976.

8. These islands are off limits to the general public.

9. Joe Kinsella, "Fogo Island—The Red Indian Connection," *Tilting Expatriate* 2 (December 1974): 10.

10. John Cardoulis, *A Friendly Invasion* (St. John's: Creative Publishers, 1993). Other United States Army radar sites in Newfoundland were located at Cape Bonavista, Torbay, St. Bride's, and Allan's Island. At one time during the war, an identification checkpoint was set up at Sandy Cove.

11. Tilting resident Annie Foley's first child was born in this hospital. She was taken to the hospital by horse and slide.

12. The Canadian army took over the base during the last year of the war.

13. One of Ben and Annie Foley's outbuildings, a store, was moved from the military base in Sandy Cove.

14. John Mannion claims the English settlement period in Tilting occurred between 1750–1780 (interview with author, 1987). Mannion's research notes indicate English settlement in Tilting on or before 1729, and he observed a marginal note to this effect on the Cook/Lane map of 1765.

15. Donald Burke, "A Short History of Tilting," *Tilting Expatriate* 1 (December 1993). Jim Greene also told me about the existence of these stones. When he was young, he was told the French used these stones to dry fish.

16. James E. Candow, "The Evolution and Impact of European Fishing Stations in the Northwest Atlantic," in Poul Holm and David J. Starkey, eds., *Studia Atlantica 3: Technological Change in the North Atlantic Fisheries, Journal of the North Atlantic Fisheries in History Association* (Esbjerg, Denmark: Centre for Maritime and Regional History, 1999), 24.

17. John Mannion, research notes on the parish records of Waterford, Ireland.

18. Michael Coady, "A Carrick Grave by Labrador Sea," letter from Newfoundland in the Irish newspaper *The Nationalist*, 16 September 1989.

19. Captain Tavenor and Archbishop James P. Howley, both quoted in Leo Moakler, "Tilton or Tilting? What's in a Name? (Excerpt from *The Barrelman*, May 4, 1950)," in *Tilting Expatriate* 1 (December 1993): 16–18.

20. G. M. Story, W. J. Kirwin, J. D. A. Widdowson, eds., *Dictionary of Newfoundland English* (Toronto: University of Toronto Press, 1982), 567, 568. The Conception Bay community's original name was The Tilts. This was later changed to Tilt Town and eventually to Tilton. There is also a Tilt Cove in Green Bay.

21. Newfoundlanders could vote either to join Canada or for local government. The vote was extremely close, and to this day it remains controversial.

22. The second car in Tilting was Ron Burke's, a 1950 Plymouth purchased in 1951. That winter, he kept it in the stable next to his horse Prince. There were no snowplows at that time.

23. Ron Burke purchased the first diesel generator in 1955, providing electricity to thirteen houses for three dollars a month.

24. Angela Kinsella and Martin Greene went along for the trip. Angela remembers tire punctures, broken fan belts, and lots of dust.

25. One of the main regulations introduced at that time was a proposed by-law against roaming animals.

26. John Kemeny (producer), *Fishermen's Meeting*. Ottawa: National Film Board of Canada, 1967. See also John Kemeny (producer), *McGraths at Home and Fishing*. Ottawa: National Film Board of Canada, 1967.

Chapter 1

1. W. J. Kirwin, G. M. Story, and P. A. O'Flaherty, eds., *Reminiscences of James P. Howley* (Toronto: Champlain Society, 1997), 111.

2. Charles Lane, interview with the author, Tilting, 1987.

3. I am indebted to James Candow for his characterization of Newfoundland's fishing stages as amphibious structures. See James E. Candow, "The Evolution and Impact of European Fishing Stations in the Northwest Atlantic," in Poul Holm and David J. Starkey, eds., *Studia Atlantica 3: Technological Change in the North Atlantic Fisheries, Journal of the North Atlantic Fisheries History Association* (Esbjerg, Denmark: Centre for Maritime and Regional History, 1999), 20.

4. F. H. A. Aalen, Kevin Whelan, and Matthew Stout, eds., *Atlas of the Irish Rural Landscape* (Toronto: University of Toronto Press, 1997), 80, 81.

5. Little Fogo Islands is a special place: islands twice removed from the main island of Newfoundland. Once inhabited year round, they form a long chain to the north of Fogo Island, and the waters are usually calm between them. There is no electricity, no litter, and no noise—just the bare rocks, seabirds, grassy meadows with wildflowers, the occasional small house and fishing stage, the church, and Cyril McGrath's sheep.

6. According to Dan Greene, the old church tower (second church) was "a wonderful mark for fishing, or anything."

7. The name France's Cove refers to the early days of fishing activity by the French in Tilting, who dried salt cod on the sand in this cove.

8. You can still see small wooden lighthouses identical to Tilting's on the north shore of Prince Edward Island in the Cavendish area.

9. Tilting has two other cemeteries: the old cemetery in Sandy Cove, with headstones dating from 1864 on, and

a new cemetery next to the road on Bunker Hill.

10. Archeologist Donald H. Holly Jr.: "Although it is likely that some form of a 'garrison' was here (a cannon survives) I was unable to identify where such a garrison may have been located.... It seems unlikely, however, that the surviving cannons were ever within the walls of a well-fortified garrison. Such a structure, if it existed, certainly would have been visible in the area's shallow soil, or ingrained in local lore. Since fortified garrison evidence is non-existent, the cannons may have merely signified a military presence in the area, perhaps associated with wooden buildings or otherwise minimal fortification. Alternatively, the cannons may derive from a shipwreck or abandoned cargo." (http://www.nfmuseum.com/977Ho.htm).

11. Jo-Anne M. Broders, "Popular Rocks," *Tilting Expatriate* 8 (December 2000), and Pearce Dwyer, interview with the author, Tilting, 1987.

12. This is the Kelly's Island branch of the same family as the Gulch branch of the Broders family, but spelled differently.

13. "Fowlue in the old usage, as in Irish Foghlu." See Michael Coady, "A Carrick Grave by Labrador Sea," letter from Newfoundland in the Irish newspaper *The Nationalist*, 16 September 1989.

14. Bonnie J. McCay, "Old People and Social Relations in a Newfoundland 'Outport,'" in Heather Strange and Michael Teitelbaum, eds., *Aging and Cultural Diversity* (South Hadley, MA: Bergen and Garvey, 1987), 61–87. On page 64, McCay describes "the postmarital virilo-cal residence and the custom of patrilineal, partible inheritance of house-sites and fishery capital."

15. Within neighborhoods, the rooms in the houses often have similar orientations. Where the length of the house corresponds with a north-south orientation, kitchens are usually placed on the south side of the house, except where priority was given to the view of the fishing premises from the kitchen, and in cases where houses had been launched to another neighborhood or turned to face the road.

16. In the 1945 census, 134 acres of land were used for agriculture: 108 acres for hay, 17 acres for potatoes, 8 acres for cabbage, and 1 acre for turnips. These produced 1817 bushels of potatoes, 281 bushels of turnip, 1,380 bushels of cabbage, and 122 tons of hay. There were 66 cows (5690 gallons of milk and 900 pounds of butter), 193 sheep (489 pounds of wool), and 8 goats. See Donald J. Greene, "Tilting," unpublished manuscript, Centre for Newfoundland Studies, Memorial University of Newfoundland Library, 1976.

17. By the late 1980s, few gardens close to the house were in use as kitchen gardens, and were instead used for growing hay, if used for agriculture at all.

18. The distinction between the front and the back of the house calls attention to the importance of the facade. Strangers and special visitors entered the front door, and neighbors entered the back door. If there was an ornamental flower garden, it would be located at the front and enclosed in a paling fence. The backyard or garden of the house was often a work area enclosed by a picket fence. When renovations were made to the exterior of the house, the front was often renovated first.

19. According to Pearce Dwyer, horses were not commonly used on Fogo Island until the early twentieth century.

20. Henry Glassie, *Passing the Time in Ballymenone* (Philadelphia: University of Pennsylvania Press, 1982). See chapter sixteen for a description of peat cutting in Ireland.

21. Juhani Pallasmaa, "Hapacity and Time: Notes on Fragile Architecture," *Architectural Review* (May 2000): 81.

Chapter 2

1. In 1987 there were 146 houses, and of these, 94 were the older type, following either the hall and parlor or center hall plan (most had a center hall plan); 44 were new (the bungalow plan far outnumbered split-level plans); and 8 were small, one-story houses with hall and parlor–type layouts, often used by seniors adjacent to their original family homes. Most of the hall and parlor–plan houses and center hall–plan houses were constructed between 1880 and 1930. Of the 94 older type houses, 45 were launched to new sites.

2. Annie Foley's mother called the steep steps in her house "the wooden hill."

3. Clarence Foley told me the change from the inside kitchen to the living room became popular in the 1940s.

4. In rural Newfoundland, the term "store" often refers to an outbuilding like a twine store, fish store, or grub store. The more common meaning of the word, a place of business, is also used for retail stores. In this case, the house was probably used as a general-purpose storage building.

5. John J. Mannion, *Irish Settlements in Eastern Canada: A Study of Cultural Transfer and Adaptation* (Toronto: University of Toronto Press, 1974). In the early 1980s, Joe Carter and I documented the Carey house in Witless Bay, Newfoundland, a full studded hall and parlor–plan house similar to Irish farmhouses described by Mannion in his book.

6. Pearce Dwyer told me his grandfather Gerald Dwyer died at age thirty-nine in 1900. Timber for his house was cut in Norris Arm in Notre Dame Bay.

7. I am indebted to Henry Glassie for these observations. Conversation with Henry Glassie, Philadelphia, 1987.

8. Gerald Pocius characterizes Newfoundland society as both hierarchical and egalitarian, and he distinguishes between egalitarian (the kitchen) and hierarchical (the parlor) realms in the folk house. He acknowledges the dominance of the egalitarian (most of the time is spent in the kitchen, and the parlor is rarely seen). See Gerald Pocius, "Hooked Rugs in Newfoundland: The Representation of Social Structure in Design," *Journal of American Folklore* 92, no. 373 (July–September, 1979): 273–284.

9. Norbert Schoenauer distinguishes between the inward-looking courtyard house of the orient and the outward-looking occidental house. Unlike the occidental house, the courtyard house presents an egalitarian exterior: the wealth and status of the occupants is not ostentatiously displayed. In the architecture of Tilting, the exterior of the house expresses the egalitarian status of the occupants. For more information on cross-cultural comparisons of house form, see Norbert Schoenauer, *6000 Years of Housing*, vols. 1–3 (New York: Garland STPM Press, 1981).

10. Leonard Broders's house had a false front door.

11. Local plan variations of standard suburban bungalows were built elsewhere in Newfoundland, such as those in Calvert. These early bungalows appeared in Calvert after Confederation in 1949, and the influence of house plans originating outside the community (such as those authored by Canada Mortgage and Housing Corporation) was not felt until after the mid-1960s. Gerald Lewis Pocius, *A Place To Belong: Community Order and Everyday Space in Calvert, Newfoundland* (Montreal: McGill Queen's University Press, 2000).

12. The Fogo Island cooperative had a positive influence on the fishery. For a detailed study of the cooperative movement on Fogo Island, see Bonnie J. McCay, "Appropriate Technology and Coastal Fishermen of Newfoundland," Ph.D. diss, Columbia University, 1976.

13. The first phase of the installation of water and sewer services was completed along the road from Tilting to Sandy Cove, a further incentive to locate a new house there. The installation of water and sewer in the main part of the community has extended all the way around the harbor to Greene's Point.

14. "When different kinds of entertainment meet, Ballymenone achieves its perfect social moment. And that is what a 'ceili' is: the conjunction of proper quiet with proper noise, the exchange of wordless and wordy gifts. In ceilis, food and stories are given, taken, traded. Ceilis are composed of neighbors who come out of the night to sit together and, as Hugh Nolan says, 'pass a lock of hours.'" Henry Glassie, *Passing the Time in Ballymenone*, (Philadelphia: University of Pennsylvania Press, 1982), 41.

15. The older generation was terrified of fire, and the fire in the stove was quenched at bedtime no matter what the weather. People were used to sleeping on warm feather mattresses with many blankets or quilts in cold rooms.

16. The Rev. Dr. E. J. Jones, the priest of St. Patrick's Parish from 1912 to 1944, had strict rules about this.

Chapter 3

1. Terry Burke told me the sills of Mike Burke's, Donovan Burke's, Herb Sexton's, John Kinsella's, and Joseph Foley's houses were laid on the same day. This is a good example of cooperation in house building in Tilting.

2. All gable roofs in Tilting had wood shingles, usually sawn in Carmanville and purchased for two dollars per bundle. All the Cape Cove houses had low-pitched felt roofs.

3. Fergus Burke told me chimneys were constructed with brick and lime mortar with sand from a place in Tilting called Trugards. Ochre powder came in red and yellow colors.

4. This is the only house in Tilting with an open fireplace (a small coal grate like the ones found in St. John's).

5. Ted Burke told me the houses in Cape Cove were painted the same way.

6. Owned at the time of this interview by Tony and Margaret Allison, and Kevin and Louise Broders.

7. Henry Glassie, interview with the author, Philadelphia, 1987. Glassie commented that he saw masonry chimneys bearing on the attic floor beams in Virginia.

8. Richard Cluett built this house around 1919. The chimney extended to ground in this house rather than resting on a mantelpiece. Each house in Cape Cove had the chimney in the center of the house and a "biscuit box," a low-pitch roof. The front exterior walls had trim boards down the middle.

Chapter 4

1. To keep horses from breaking through the gate at night or when no one was home, a two-by-four embedded with nails was often placed between the gate posts at the top of the gate.

2. Pearce told me that 7:30–9:00 P.M. was the bedtime for children. When he was sixteen years old, Pearce was punished for coming in after 9:00 P.M. He had to leave Tilting to start teaching in Cape St. Georges on the west coast of Newfoundland in September of that year, so he kept no curfew hours after that. Pearce was not allowed to go to the neighboring outport of Joe Batt's Arm until he was sixteen years old.

3. These early septic systems were mostly cesspits, without proper drainage fields for filtered distribution of effluents. Cold temperatures, poor soil cover, and heavy frost retarded the biological action on sewage. Water and sewer service has now reached most families in Tilting, but it remains to be seen if a sewage treatment plant will ever get installed. Very few

Newfoundland communities can afford to treat their sewage before discharging it to the open ocean.

4. Glassie described three zones for Ballymenone's kitchen dressers: the useful or lowest zone that hides utilitarian items like pots and pans, the social or middle zone, offering hospitality to visitors—a counter for tea pots and tea cups and other items used every day, and the highest zone hosting a beautiful display of special dishes and souvenirs. Henry Glassie, material folk culture seminar, University of Pennsylvania, 1985.

5. Thinking about ornamental furniture carving in Tilting, I remembered John Ruskin's observation of Venetian boat ornament. For Ruskin, the carving on these boats expressed the germ of ornament: the human instinct to hack at an edge. John Ruskin, *The Stones of Venice* (London: Smith, Elder, 1851–53), 259.

6. Earle's was known locally as Bryan's. P. J. Bryan and his son Herbert ran the company before Kinsella.

7. John Power's wife. They lived in the small saltbox-roofed house near the road to Oliver's Cove described earlier.

Chapter 5

1. It is possible that these same residents would have had less difficulty identifying outbuildings during a walk through the community, instead of relying on photographs.

2. Bryan McKay-Lyons compared the framing of houses in Nova Scotia to bones and the cladding to forgiving, elastic skin. Bryan McKay-Lyons, lecture, St. John's, 1989.

3. This hen house was five by three feet in area and three feet high with a "one-sided" roof. It had a little door with an eight-by-ten-inch window. Dan Greene, interview with the author, Tilting, 1988. Dan's chickens were free-range, except in winter.

4. This hen house is now behind Roy Dwyer's house. Originally, it was on the Kinsella premises in the yard between the house and the attached outbuildings.

5. Bonnie J. McCay, "Fish Guts, Hair Nets, and Unemployment Stamps," in Peter Sinclair, ed., *A Question of Survival: The Fisheries and Newfoundland Society* (St. John's: I.S.E.R., Memorial University, 1989), 172.

6. William J. Kirwin, G. M. Story, and Patrick A. O'Flaherty, eds., *Reminiscences of James P. Howley: Selected Years* (Toronto: Champlain Society, 1997), 109.

7. James Candow, "The Evolution and Impact of European Fishing Stations in the Northwest Atlantic," in *Studia Atlantica 3: Technological Change in the North Atlantic Fisheries, Journal of the North Atlantic Fisheries History Association* (Esbjerg, Denmark: Centre for Maritime and Regional History, 1999): 28.

Chapter 6

1. James Candow described the antecedents of fishing stages in Newfoundland. These relate to the early phase of Newfoundland's fishery, the shore station of the migratory fishery. "The four main components of the shore station were the stage, an elongated and partially enclosed wooden structure that extended from the land out over the water, where the fish was landed, gutted, headed, split and salted; the beach or flake (raised wooden platform) where fish was laid to dry; cabins or houses for the work crews and officers; and the cookroom, where the men ate and sometimes slept if separate houses did not exist for that purpose. The stage and flake were known by name as early as 1577....The shore stations of the inshore fishery have had a profound influence along Canada's Atlantic littoral." James E. Candow, "The Evolution and Impact of European Fishing Stations in the Northwest

Atlantic," in *Studia Atlantica 3: Technological Change in the North Atlantic Fisheries*, *Journal of the North Atlantic Fisheries History Association* (Esbjerg, Denmark: Centre for Maritime and Regional History, 1999): 11, 12.

2. Boat dimensions were as follows: small row punt: sixteen feet long, four feet wide, twenty-two inches deep; trap skiff: twenty to thirty feet long (Fergus Burke's was twenty-eight feet long, seven feet wide, forty-five inches deep); bully boat: thirty to thirty-three feet long, eight feet wide, forty-eight inches deep. Bully boats were used for fishing in the fall of the year on the "offer" grounds (offshore grounds where there were shoals). They were also used to "cruise wood" (transport wood) from the bay to Fogo Island, and for transport when families would sometimes move to bay communities like Norris Arm for the winter.

3. Candow, "Evolution and Impact," 20.

4. Professor Gerald Pocius documented Dan Greene's fishing stage in Tilting in the early 1990s. For more detailed information on this and other fishing stages on Fogo Island see Gerald Pocius, "The House that Jack Poor Built: Architectural Stages in the Newfoundland Fishery" in Larrie McCann and Carrie MacMillan, eds., *The Sea and Culture in Atlantic Canada: A Multidisciplinary Sampler* (Sackville: Centre for Canadian Studies, Mount Allison University, 1992), 64–105.

5. The stages that remain on Little Fogo Islands are used only seasonally and are difficult to maintain, so the strouters (wide ladders from the stage to the water) are retracted and placed on the land when not in use. In addition to fishing stages and houses, there is a small Catholic church that was recently restored with original materials (painted wood exterior and painted wood shingles) in the central part of Little Fogo. On August 15, the date of the Feast of the Immaculate

Conception, residents from Tilting, Joe Batt's Arm, and other Fogo Island communities travel to Little Fogo to celebrate a mass. The church vestibule has signatures from visitors from all over the world, many from those visiting Little Fogo Islands by sailboat.

6. In the short bulk pounds, dividing boards were installed after every three feet of fish was filled (five feet high). These pounds held about twenty quintals of fish in each tier. If the fishing was good, two or three pounds could be filled in a day. After the fish packed down from shrinkage, more could be added. The long bulk pound was used earlier, and could hold twice the amount of fish.

7. The top floor of Dan Greene's old twine store (now removed) was used for storing nets, sails, and rope. Boat hooks, spars, grapelins, buckets, the punt, and paddles were kept in the stage. The first floor of his twine store was used for a workshop. Work on fishing gear commenced in the twine store loft at the end of March or the beginning of April. There was no time before that because of slide hauling.

8. Jim Greene, interview with the author, Titling, 1987.

Chapter 7

1. There is some confusion about the correct term for this building. Frank Mahoney told me in Tilting they were called stables rather than barns.

2. Allan Keefe, interview with the author, Tilting, 1987. A "square" of cabbage is six feet square.

3. Turnips were given the same treatment as cabbage, an eighteen-inch spacing for the seed. Turnips were harvested after sixty days. The roots and leaves were cut off with a knife. After drying for a couple of days, they were placed in the root cellar.

Chapter 8

1. This project is the 2001 restoration of Vincent Bryan's premises, constructed in the early 1890s and purchased by Albert Dwyer in 1925. The buildings include the house, stage, twine, store, and flake. Kyran Burke and his sons Cyril, Tom, and Louis were the original owners of the twine store.

GLOSSARY OF LOCAL TERMS

BALLICADER: Sheet of ice forming along the ocean shores in winter

BALLAST LOCKER: Partially submerged, heavy timber, log-cabin-type frame encasing large, loose stones for a stage or bridge wharf

BARKING POT: Pots used to "bark" or preserve the cotton twine of the traditional cod trap

BAWN: Grassy mound or area: a vacant piece of land owned by a family

BOUGHING: Marking a slide path where it crosses the pond with boughs in winter

BRIDGE: Raised wooden platform providing access to an outbuilding or to a house

BULK: Enclosure (a pound) in a fishing stage used for curing salt fish

BULLY BOAT: Boat used for freight and transport, mainly after the schooner era

BUNGALOW: One-story, rectangular house, sometimes called a ranch house elsewhere in Newfoundland

CHIFFONIER: Sideboard kept in either the kitchen or "the room" of the old house

COOPED: Ceiling that does not allow full headroom along an exterior wall because of the imposition of the roof (also, "coped")

COUCH: Piece of furniture commonly found in the kitchen of the folk house that allowed either a reclining or sitting posture; they could be either single or double headed

COUPLE: Pair of rafters for a gable roof

COW HUNTING: Searching for cows grazing in open fields and scrub land so that they can be milked

CRANNICK: Crooked, "boxy" (knotty) wood used for firewood

DIETERS: Men who received room and board in exchange for helping a fisherman

DOUGHBOYS: Dumplings made with flour

DROKE: Ridge of stunted woods

FLAKE: Raised wooden platform used for drying fish

GALLERY: Landmark such as an outcrop of rock used as a gathering place; bridge leading to the door of a house

HEIGHT: Raised ground, as in a hill along a slide path

HOUSE LAUNCHING: House moving, from one community to another or within a community

INSIDE KITCHEN: Original kitchen located in the main part of an old house

JUNK: Cut wood in stove-length pieces

KILLICK: Anchor made by encasing a heavy stone in a light wooden cage

LAUNCH: To move a house or outbuilding, analogous to launching a boat

LEAD: Passageway across marshy ground

LINNET: Net

LONGER: Wood (in the round) of an intermediate size used for braces, fences, bedding flakes, bridges, boughing, and tools

LUN: Sheltered spot out of the wind, as on the side of a hill

MANTELPIECE: Heavy, dressed timber used to support a masonry chimney in an old house

MEADOW: Fenced-in grass area (could also refer to a garden)

NECK: Strip of woods between two ponds or two marshes

NUDDICK: Small hill

OUTPORT: Small, at times isolated, Newfoundland coastal community, often inaccessible by road

PASS: Narrow passage in a slide path

PIGGIN: Tool used to bail out a boat—the handle could be carved or made from barrel staves

PINCH: Hill or rise in a slide path

PIT SAW: Saw used by two persons in a twine store (one upstairs, one downstairs) for ripping boards

POTATO TRENCHING: Fertilizing potato beds with
    capelin

POTLIDS: Homemade snowshoes made from flat boards

POOK: Mound of hay weighing about two hundred
    pounds

POUND: Enclosure made from boards, such as that used
    for confining animals in a stable or for curing salt
    fish in a fishing stage

QUARRY: Condition where there is water on top of ice,
    produced when water flows up from under ice

QUINTAL: Hundredweight (112 pounds) measure of
    cod fish

RIDGE: Rise in the land, such as a long hill. Usually, a
    slide path does not cross a ridge

RIND: Remove bark from a log with an axe

ROOM: Formal room in the old house used for entertain-
    ing strangers, for wakes, or for displaying
    special family possessions

ROW PUNT: Small row boat

SCOFF: Large, special meal attended by many persons

SCOURGE: Pester someone by making demands or
    requesting favors

SETTLE: Kitchen couch, usually homemade with
    minimal upholstery

SKID: Long beam used as a sled runner in house launching

STRINGER: Purlin

SHANTY LOFT: Top floor of a twine store used for
    sharemen's accommodations in summer

SHAREMEN: Men assisting in the fishery who obtain a
    share of the catch

SLIDE HAULING: Harvesting wood using a horse
    and slide

SLIDE PATH: Path used in winter for hauling wood

SLOB WEATHER: High winds and cold temperatures
    at the onset of winter

SPELL: Short distance or taking a rest while working;
    also, working over a short distance, such as carry-

ing a heavy turn of wood

SPUDGEL: Small wooden bucket used for bailing water
    and other tasks

SPAR SHORE: Shore placed at an angle on the outside
    of a fishing stage to counter the force of the load of
    salt fish curing in bulks or pounds

STAGE: Outbuilding used for storing gear and process-
    ing fish, located along the shore

STAMPED MAT: Mat made from a purchased pattern

STORE: Outbuilding used for storage

STRONGBACK: Heavy ridge beam for a gable roof–
    type structure or a wood pile

STROUTER: Longer used as a ladder on a fishing stage

SWAB: Stick with a rag nailed onto the end used for
    washing down a boat or a stage

TEAR: Energetic person who gets a lot of work done

TILT: Temporary wooden gable-roofed structure with
    vertical studding, whose roof is sometimes
    covered with sods

TOUTON: Pan-cooked bread dough

TRAP BERTH: Near-shore location for setting cod
    fishing traps

TRAP SKIFF: Fishing boat used for hauling cod traps

TURN: Quantity of wood or water that can be carried by
    one person

TWINE STORE: Outbuilding associated with the
    fishery, usually with a loft for mending nets on the
    second floor

UPRIGHT: Wall stud in a house or outbuilding

WATER HOOP: Device used to balance water buckets
    while hauling water from a well

WINDOW LEAVES: Double doors located in the stage
    head area of a fishing stage, designed to avoid
    being caught by the wind

*I am indebted to Fergus Burke for his contribution
to this glossary.*

BIBLIOGRAPHY

Aalen, F. H. A., Kevin Whelan, and Matthew Stout, eds. *Atlas of the Irish Rural Landscape* (Toronto: University of Toronto Press, 1997).

Armstrong, Robert Plant. *The Affecting Presence: An Essay in Humanistic Anthropology* (Urbana: University of Illinois Press, 1971).

Burke, Donald. "A Short History of Tilting." *Tilting Expatriate* 1 (December 1993).

Broders, Jo-Anne M. "Popular Rocks." *Tilting Expatriate* 8 (December 2000).

Candow, James E. and Carol Corbin, eds. *How Deep is the Ocean?: Historical Essays on Canada's Atlantic Fishery* (Sydney: University of Cape Breton Press, 1997).

Candow, James E. "The Evolution and Impact of European Fishing Stations in the Northwest Atlantic." In *Studia Atlantica 3: Technological Change in the North Atlantic Fisheries, Journal of the North Atlantic Fisheries History Association* (Esbjerg, Denmark: Centre for Maritime and Regional History, 1999).

Cardoulis, John. *A Friendly Invasion* (St. John's: Creative Publishers, 1993).

Conrad, Margaret R. and James Hiller. *Atlantic Canada: Region in the Making* (New York: Oxford University Press, 2001).

Coady, Michael. "A Carrick Grave by Labrador Sea." Letter from Newfoundland in the Irish newspaper *The Nationalist*, 16 September 1989.

Evans, E. Estyn. *The Personality of Ireland: Habitat, Heritage and History* (Cambridge: Cambridge University Press, 1973).

Gailey, Alan. *Rural Houses in the North of Ireland* (Edinburgh: John Donald Publishers, 1984).

Glassie, Henry. "Archaeology and Folklore: Common Anxieties, Common Hopes." In Leland Ferguson, ed. *Historical Archaeology and the Importance of Things* (Society for Historical Archaeology, 1977).

————. *Folk Housing in Middle Virginia* (Knoxville: University of Tennessee Press, 1975).

————. *Passing the Time in Ballymenone* (Philadelphia: University of Pennsylvania Press, 1982).

————. *Pattern in the Material Folk Culture of the Eastern United States* (Philadelphia: University of Pennsylvania Press, 1968).

————. "Structure and Function, Folklore and the Artifact." *Semiotica* 7: 4 (1973): 331–351.

————. *The Spirit of Folk Art* (New York: Abrams, 1989).

————. *Vernacular Architecture* (Bloomington: Indiana University Press, 2000).

————. "Vernacular Architecture and Society." *Material Culture* 16: 4 (1984): 4–21.

Greene, Donald J. "Tilting." Photocopy of unpublished manuscript, Center for Newfoundland Studies, Memorial University of Newfoundland Library, 1976.

Handcock, W. Gordon. *So Longe as there comes noe women: Origins of English Settlement in Newfoundland* (St. John's: Breakwater Books, 1989).

Holl, Steven. *Rural and Urban House Types in North America: Pamphlet Architecture* 9 (New York: Princeton Architectural Press, 1982).

Kemeny, John (producer). *Fishermen's Meeting*. Ottawa: National Film Board of Canada, 1967.

————. *McGraths at Home and Fishing*. Ottawa: National Film Board of Canada, 1967.

King, Anthony. "The Bungalow." *Architectural Association Quarterly* 5: 3 (1973).

Kinsella, Joe. "Fogo Island—The Red Indian Connection." *Tilting Expatriate* 2 (December 1974): 10.

Kirwin, William J., G. M. Story, and Patrick A. O'Flaherty, eds. *Reminiscences of James P. Howley: Selected Years* (Toronto: Champlain Society, 1997).

Kubler, George. *The Shape of Time* (New Haven: Yale University Press, 1962).

Mannion, John J. *Irish Settlements in Eastern Canada: A Study of Cultural Transfer and Adaptation* (Toronto: University of Toronto Press, 1974).

McCann, Larry with Carrie MacMillan. *The Sea and Culture of Atlantic Canada* (Sackville, New Brunswick: Centre for Canadian Studies, Mount Allison University, 1992).

McCay, Bonnie J. "Appropriate Technology and Coastal Fishermen of Newfoundland." Ph.D. diss., Columbia University, 1976.

————. "Fish Guts, Hair Nets, and Unemployment Stamps." In Peter Sinclair, ed. *A Question of Survival: The Fisheries and Newfoundland Society* (St. John's: I.S.E.R., Memorial University, 1989), 172.

————. "Old People and Social Relations in a Newfoundland 'Outport.'" In *Aging and Cultural Diversity*. Heather Strange and Michele Teitelbaum, eds. (South Hadley, MA: Bergen & Garvey, 1987).

————. "Fish is Scarce: Fisheries Modernization on Fogo Island, Newfoundland." In Raoul Anderson, ed. *North Atlantic Maritime Cultures* (The Hague: Mouton, 1979), 155–188.

McCleary, Peter. "Structure and Intuition." *A.I.A. Journal* (October 1980): 56–119.

Mednis, Roberts Janis. "A Phytogeographical Analysis of the Occurrence of Vegetation Patterns on Fogo Island, Newfoundland-Labrador." Ph.D. diss., Boston University, 1971.

Messenger, John. C. *Inis Beag: Isle of Ireland* (New York: Holt, Rinehart and Winston, 1969).

Mills, David B. "The Evolution of Folk House Forms in Trinity Bay, Newfoundland." M.A. thesis, Memorial University of Newfoundland, 1975.

Moakler, Leo. "Tilton or Tilting? What's in a Name? (Excerpt from *The Barrelman*, May 4, 1950)." In *Tilting Expatriate* 1 (December 1993): 16–18.

Newell, Dianne and Rosemary E. Ommer, eds. *Fishing Places and Fishing People: Traditions and Issues in Canadian Small-Scale Fisheries* (Toronto: University of Toronto Press, 1999).

Oliver, Basil. *The Cottages of England: A Review of Their Types and Features from the 16th to the 18th Centuries* (London: B. T. Batsford, 1929).

Pallasmaa, Juhani. "Hapacity and Time: Notes on Fragile Architecture." *Architectural Review* (May 2000): 78–84.

Peck, R. M. "The Incidence of False Windows in Two Early Newfoundland Lighthouses." *APT Bulletin* 9: 1 (1977): 4–10.

Pocius, Gerald Lewis. "Architecture on Newfoundland's Southern Shore: Diversity and the Emergence of New World Forms." *Perspectives in Vernacular Architecture* (Williamsburg: Vernacular Architecture Forum, 1982), 217–232.

————. *A Place to Belong: Community Order and Everyday Space in Calvert, Newfoundland* (Montreal: McGill Queen's University Press, 2000).

————. "Gossip, Rhetoric, and Objects: A Sociolinguistic Approach to Newfoundland Furniture." *Perspectives on American Furniture* (New York: W. W. Norton & Company, 1988), 303–345.

————. "Hooked Rugs in Newfoundland: The Representation of Social Structure in Design." *Journal of American Folklore* 92: 373 (July–September 1979): 273–284.

————. "The House that Jack Poor Built: Architectural Stages in the Newfoundland Fishery." In L. McCann and C. MacMillan, eds. *The Sea and Culture in Atlantic Canada: A Multidisciplinary Sampler* (Sackville, New Brunswick: Centre for Canadian Studies, Mount Allison University, 1992), 64–105.

Ruskin, John. *The Seven Lamps of Architecture* (New York: Farrar, Straus and Giroux, 1981).

————. *The Stones of Venice* (London: Smith, Elder, 1851–53).

St. George, Robert Blair. *Conversing by Signs; Poetics of Implication in Colonial New England Culture* (Chapel Hill: University of North Carolina Press, 1998).

————. *Material Life in America, 1600–1800* (Boston: Northeastern University Press, 1988).

Schoenauer, Norbert. *6000 Years of Housing*. Vols. 1–3 (New York: Garland STPM Press, 1981).

Story, G. M. and W. J. Kirwin, J. D. A. Widdowson. *Dictionary of Newfoundland English* (Toronto: University of Toronto Press, 1982).

Vitruvius. *On Architecture*, ed. Frank Granger (Cambridge: Harvard University Press, 1970)

INDEX

page numbers of images are set in italics

McGrath, Andrew, 47, 56, 118, *193*
McGrath, Austin, 160
McGrath, Billy, 160
McGrath, Cyril, 35, *47*, 118, *189*, *193*
McGrath, Ed, 67, 118
McGrath, Frank, 47, 118
McGrath, Gerard, *22*, 132
McGrath, Gladys, *25*, 56, 118, *119*
McGrath, Harold, *22*, 146, 178
McGrath, Jill, *22*, *78*, *119*
McGrath, Jim, 14, *193*
McGrath, Justin, 140
McGrath, Len, 67, 118
McGrath, Leo, 47, 118
McGrath, Margaret, 132
McGrath, Mary Claire, *22*
McGrath, Michael (Sr.), 178
McGrath, Mike, 78, 160
McGrath, Neil, *25*, 56, *57*
McGrath, Ray, 181
McGrath, William, 221
Meadow, The, 190
meals, 121, 125
Mellin, Hannah, *22*
Mellin, Hetti, *165*
Mellin, Julia, *22*
Mickel's Pond, 56
Middle Point, 39
Mik Keefe's Point, 38
milk houses, 136, *139*, 143, 145, *148*, *150*
moose, 61
Morris Lyon's Cove Hills, 64
motorboats. *See* boats: motorboats
mummers, 85, 93
Murray's Island, 36
Nance's Point, 160
Nap, The, 46
naps, 118, 130
National Film Board, 23
neighborhoods, 36, 37, 40, 46–47, 49
Norris Arm, 17
O'Brien, Father Edward Joseph, 18
O'Brien, Father Joseph M., 14
ochre, 105, 108, 140

Oliver's Cove, 6, 30, *32*, 37–38, *39*, 61, 64, 79–80, 139, 159–160, 186, 190, 197–199, 206, 209
Oliver's Cove Head, 37–38
outbuildings, 2, 50, 136–153, 224: attached, 140, 142; for agriculture, 184–210; construction of, 142; for the fishery, 156–181; gender domains, 149; identification, 138; launching, 140, 223; location, 48–49; materials, 148; ownership, 136, 138, 140; painted ornaments, 140, *147*, 163; painting, 140, *142*; purpose, 48–51, 136, 148; reconstruction, 223; roofs, 138, 142; size, 136, 140
outhouses, 136, *138*
Pad Keefe's Point, 160
paling fence. *See* fences: paling
Palmer's, 64
peat, 59, 61
Penton, Peter, 223
Penton, Tim, 223
Peter's Cove, 115
picket fence. *See* fences: picket
pig pounds, 136, 146
Pigeon Island, 2, 28, 40, 160
Pinch, The, 190
pit saw, 96, 104, 177
place names, 38–40, 41, 46
polar bears, 9
Pond, The, *vi*, *12*, 15, 17, 28, 30, *91*
Pond Tickle, 36
population, 53
post office, 35, *36*
Potato Hole Point, 38
potato trenching, 207
Power, Cecilia, 131
Pummely Cove, 39
Pummely Cove Point, 39
Pummely Cove Pond, 39, 61
rafting, *30*
Raggedy Nuddick, 38
Reardon, Bridget, 121, 142

Reardon, Edith, vii, 24, 94, 122
Reardon, Elsie, 92
Reardon, Gerald, 70, 72–95, 223
Reardon, Greg, 110, 121
Reardon, Jack, 72–95
Reardon, Pat, 160
Reardon's Island, 46, 222–223
regulations (by-laws), 19, 33–34, 191
riddle fence. *See* fences: riddle
roads, 31, 164
religion, 18, 20
Rock, The, 28, *31*, 36–37, 44, *45*, 46, *51*, 64, 71, 106–107, 111, 130, 140–141, 156, 162, 192, 224: mercantile premises on, 44, 46; Rock Bridge, 31
Rock in the Garden, 31
Rock of the Head, 38, 160
root cellars, 33, 37, 136, 149, 184, 194, *195*–*199*, 207
Round Head, 52, 139, 160, 162
row punts. *See* boats: row punts
St. Patrick's Parish, 2, 35: Parish Club, 20, 35, 37; Parish Hall, *37*; Parish House, *18*, *35*; second church, 2, 17, *18*, 35; third church, *35*
salmon. *See* fish: salmon
salt fish. *See* fish: salt fish
Sand Cove Forest, 80
Sandy Cove, 9–10, 26, 30, 32, *33*, 50, 70, *72*–*94*, *95*, 140–141, 186, 192, 202, 206, 215: fences, 9; gardens in, 9; history, 9; houses, 9; location, 6; outbuildings, 9
Sandy Cove beach, 9, 121, 158
Sandy Cove Bight, 61, 165
Sandy Cove Hill, 196
Sandy Cove Pond, 64, 108
Sandy Lookout, 204
Saunders, Alonzo, *58*
Saunders, Fred, 146
Saunders, Lambert, 129–130
Saunders, Solomon, 104